ADMINISTRATIVE LAW

Second Edition

Jack M. Beermann
Professor of Law, Boston University School of Law

The *CrunchTime* Series

PUBLISHERS

76 Ninth Avenue, New York, NY 10011
http://lawschool.aspenpublishers.com

Printed in the United States of America.

ISBN 0-7355-5860-4

1 2 3 4 5 6 7 8 9 0

This book is intended as a general review of a legal subject. It is not intended as a source for advice for the solution of legal matters or problems. For advice on legal matters, the reader should consult an attorney.

About Aspen Publishers

Aspen Publishers, headquartered in New York City, is a leading information provider for attorneys, business professionals, and law students. Written by preeminent authorities, our products consist of analytical and practical information covering both U.S. and international topics. We publish in the full range of formats, including updated manuals, books, periodicals, CDs, and online products.

Our proprietary content is complemented by 2,500 legal databases, containing over 11 million documents, available through our Loislaw division. Aspen Publishers also offers a wide range of topical legal and business databases linked to Loislaw's primary material. Our mission is to provide accurate, timely, and authoritative content in easily accessible formats, supported by unmatched customer care.

To order any Aspen Publishers title, go to *http://lawschool.aspenpublishers.com* or call 1-800-638-8437.

To reinstate your manual update service, call 1-800-638-8437.

For more information on Loislaw products, go to *www.loislaw.com* or call 1-800-364-2512.

For Customer Care issues, e-mail *CustomerCare@aspenpublishers.com*; call 1-800-234-1660; or fax 1-800-901-9075.

Aspen Publishers
a Wolters Kluwer business

Summary of Contents

Table of Contents

FLOW CHARTS

CAPSULE SUMMARY

EXAM TIPS

Preface

Thank you for buying this book.

The *CrunchTime* Series is intended for people who want Emanuel quality but don't have the time to buy and use the full-length *Emanuel Law Outline* on a subject. We've designed the Series to be used in the last few weeks (or even less) before your final exams.

This book includes the following features, most of which have been extracted from the corresponding *Emanuel Law Outline:*

- ■ *Flow Charts* — We've reduced many of the principles of *Administrative Law* to a series of 13 flow charts, created specially for this book and never published elsewhere. We think these will be especially useful on open-book exams. The flow charts begin on p. 1.

- ■ *Capsule Summary* — This is a 30-page or so summary of the subject. We've carefully crafted it to cover the things you're most likely to be asked on an exam. The Capsule Summary starts on p. 37.

- ■ *Exam Tips* — We've compiled these by reviewing dozens of actual past essay and multiple-choice questions asked in past law-school and bar exams, extracting the issues and "tricks" that surface most often on exams. The Exam Tips start on p. 73.

- ■ *Short-Answer Questions and Answers* — These questions are generally in a yes/no format, with a "mini-essay" explaining each one. The questions start on p. 95.

- ■ *Essay Questions and Answers* — These questions are actual ones asked on law school exams. They start on p. 129.

We hope you find this book helpful and instructive.

Good luck.

Jack M. Beermann
Boston, Massachusetts
May 2006

FLOW CHARTS

FLOW CHARTS

SUMMARY OF CONTENTS

APPOINTMENT OF ADMINISTRATIVE OFFICIALS

Use this chart to analyze the constitutionality of the appoinment of federal officials.

Start here

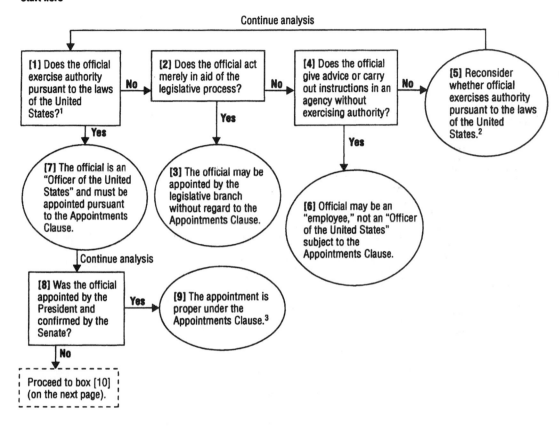

FIGURE 1 (*cont.*)

APPOINTMENT OF ADMINISTRATIVE OFFICIALS

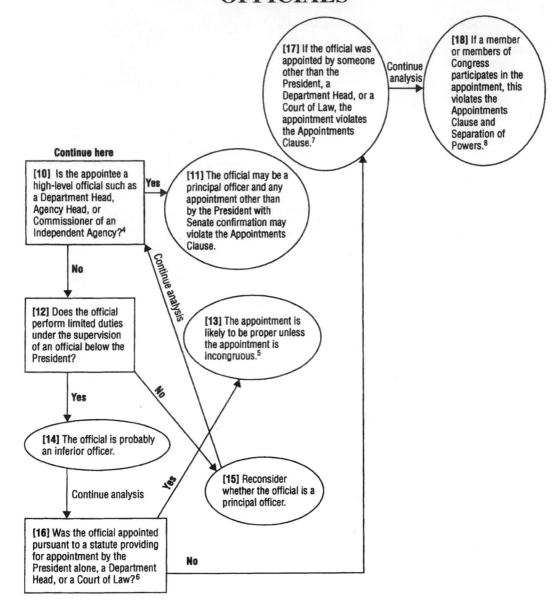

[17] If the official was appointed by someone other than the President, a Department Head, or a Court of Law, the appointment violates the Appointments Clause.[7]

Continue analysis →

[18] If a member or members of Congress participates in the appointment, this violates the Appointments Clause and Separation of Powers.[8]

Continue here

[10] Is the appointee a high-level official such as a Department Head, Agency Head, or Commissioner of an Independent Agency?[4]

Yes →

[11] The official may be a principal officer and any appointment other than by the President with Senate confirmation may violate the Appointments Clause.

No ↓

Continue analysis

[12] Does the official perform limited duties under the supervision of an official below the President?

[13] The appointment is likely to be proper unless the appointment is incongruous.[5]

Yes ↓

No

[14] The official is probably an inferior officer.

Continue analysis

Yes

[15] Reconsider whether the official is a principal officer.

[16] Was the official appointed pursuant to a statute providing for appointment by the President alone, a Department Head, or a Court of Law?[6]

No

NOTES TO FIGURE 1

APPOINTMENT OF ADMINISTRATIVE OFFICIALS

[1] This is the standard for determining whether an official is an "Officer of the United States" who may be appointed only pursuant to the Appointments Clause. *See Buckley v. Valeo.*

[2] There are two categories of federal officials to whom the Appointments Clause does not apply: those acting merely in aid of the legislative process (who may be appointed by Congress or a subset of its members) and those who have no actual authority but rather are merely government "employees." A federal official not in one of those two categories is probably an Officer of the United States to whom the Appointments Clause applies.

[3] Absent legislation to the contrary, the model in the Appointments Clause for appointing all Officers of the United States is appointment by the President and confirmation by the Senate. See U.S. Const., Art. II, §2, cl. 2.

[4] High-level officials such as Department Heads and Independent Agency Commissioners are "Principal" or "Superior" Officers, and they must be appointed by the President with Senate confirmation. If an official has limited responsibilities and is under the supervision of an executive branch official below the President, the official is probably an Inferior Officer for whom the Appointments Clause allows an alternative method of appointment. *See Morrison v. Olson, Edmond v. United States.*

[5] The Supreme Court has stated that a statute providing for the appointment of an inferior officer by someone other than the President may be void if there is incongruity between the identity of the appointing official and the duties of the appointee, for example, if Congress designates the Secretary of the Interior as the official with authority to appoint Assistant United States Attorneys.

[6] The Appointments Clause allows Congress to specify by statute that Inferior Officers may be appointed by the President alone, by a Department Head, or by a Court of Law. In the absence of such a statute, presidential appointment with Senate confirmation is required.

[7] Only those officials named in the Appointments Clause may participate in the appointment of inferior officers.

[8] As a corollary to the note above, because Congress or any subset of Congress is not named in the Appointments Clause, a member or members of Congress may not participate in the appointment of Inferior Officers. In addition, it probably would violate separation of powers for Congress to participate in the appointment of Executive Branch officials.

REMOVAL OF EXECUTIVE OFFICIALS

Use this chart to analyze whether restrictions on the removal of officers of the United States are constitutional.

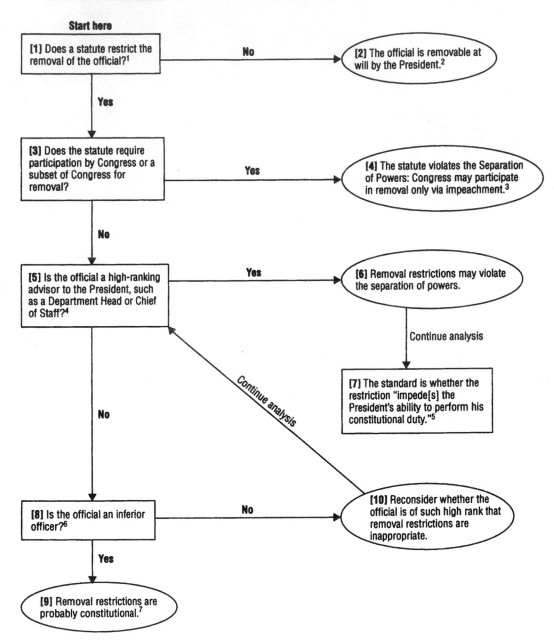

REMOVAL OF EXECUTIVE OFFICIALS

[1] The typical removal restriction provides that an official may not be removed except for good cause. Good cause is often defined as "inefficiency, neglect of duty or malfeasance in office." Some officials are appointed for a term of years and are subject to removal for cause or when their terms expire.

[2] There may be non-separation of powers limits on the ability to discharge officials, such as First Amendment concerns. These are not considered in this chart. Also, the situation of low-level civil service employees is not considered here, only officials considered "Officers of the United States."

[3] *Myers v. United States.*

[4] This question roughly describes the category of officials known as principal or superior officers.

[5] *Morrison v. Olson.* The standard announced in *Morrison* repudiates the Court's view in *Humphrey's Executor* that removal restrictions were justified only when the official performed quasi-legislative and quasi-judicial functions.

[6] Officers of the United States who are under the supervision of officials below the President and whose duties are limited are "inferior officers" under the Appointments Clause. Removal restrictions regarding such officials are likely, after *Morrison,* to be upheld.

[7] The Court in *Morrison* did allow for the possibility, harkening back to *Humphrey's Executor* and *Myers,* that restrictions on removing officials performing purely executive functions may be unconstitutional, but in *Morrison* itself, the Court upheld restrictions on the removal of a prosecutor, the purest of executive functions.

FIGURE 3

AVAILABILITY OF JUDICIAL REVIEW

Use this chart to determine whether an agency action is reviewable.

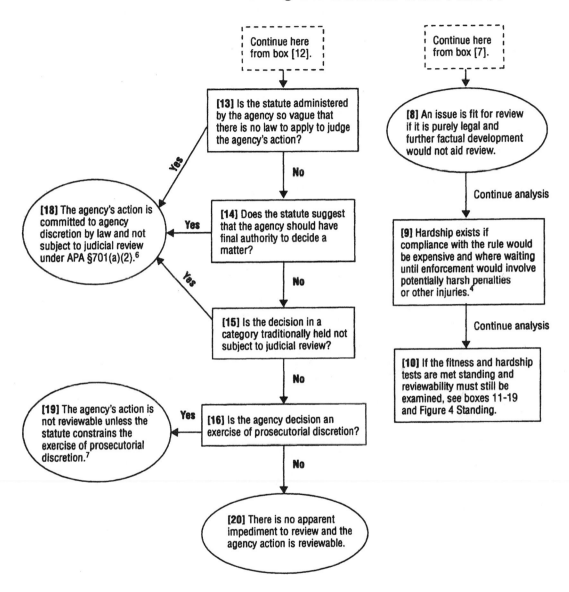

FIGURE 3 *(cont.)*

AVAILABILITY OF JUDICIAL REVIEW

AVAILABILITY OF JUDICIAL REVIEW

[1] APA §704 states that "agency action made reviewable by statute" is reviewable.

[2] APA §704 states that "final agency action for which there is no adequate remedy in a court" is reviewable.

[3] *See Abbott Laboratories v. Gardner.*

[4] *Id.*

[5] For a statute to preclude judicial review, it must mention judicial review and either preclude it altogether or channel review to a method of review different from the one being sought in the case under consideration. For example, the statute in *McNary v. Haitian Refugee Center, Inc.,* channeled review of the denial of a special immigrant worker status to review of orders of deportation, thus precluding any other form of review of the denial of the special status. Note also that in the *McNary* case, the Court held that the preclusion of review of individual denials did not preclude review of a general challenge to the administration of the program.

[6] *See Citizens to Preserve Overton Park v. Volpe. Overton Park* stated that agency action was committed to agency discretion by law when there was "no law to apply." The Supreme Court later expanded the definition of "committed to agency discretion by law" to include statutory language indicating that the agency has final authority in *Webster v. Doe.* In *Lincoln v. Vigil,* the Court made a further expansion, recognizing that some agency actions are "committed to agency discretion by law" because they are in a category of agency action in which review has traditionally been unavailable. These include prosecutorial discretion and allocation of funds from a lump sum appropriation.

[7] *See Heckler v. Chaney.*

FIGURE 4

STANDING

Use this chart to analyze whether a particular plaintiff has standing.

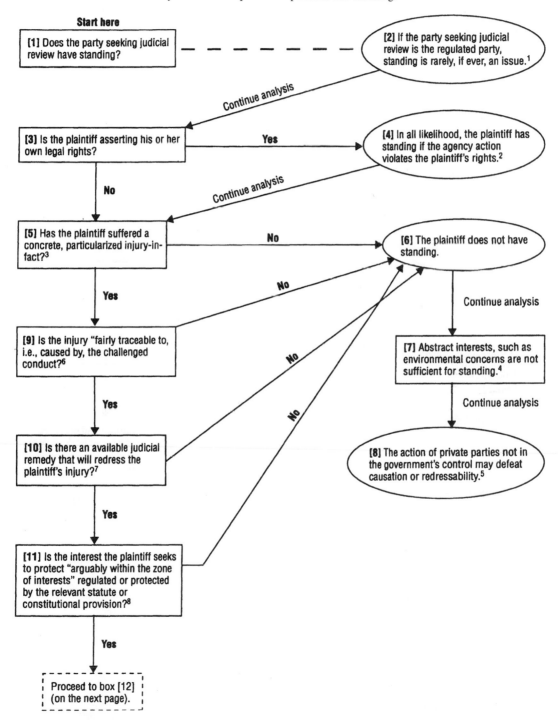

FIGURE 4 (*cont.*)

STANDING

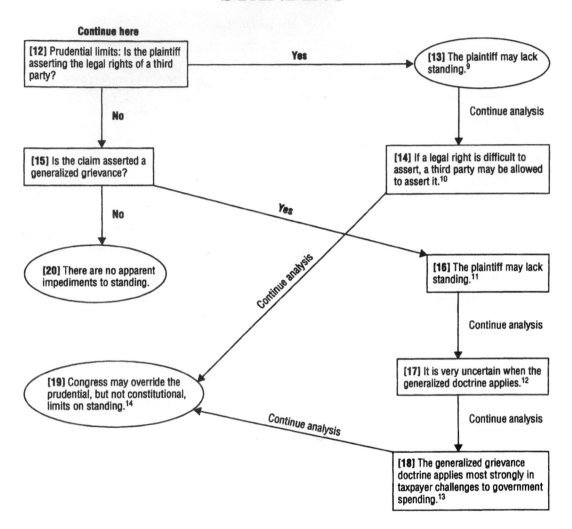

NOTES TO FIGURE 4
STANDING

[1] The traditional test for standing required that the plaintiff be asserting his or her own legal right against the challenged government action. *Association of Data Processing Service Organizations v. Camp* expanded standing beyond these limits but did not affect the standing of those within the traditional core.

[2] APA §702 provides standing to "a person suffering legal wrong because of agency action." Standing is rarely an issue if an agency has violated the plaintiffs own legal rights.

[3] The most authoritative relatively recent statement of constitutional standing requirements is *Lujan v. Defenders of Wildlife.* The basic standing requirements (injury, causation and redressability) are all stated and analyzed in that case.

[4] *See Sierra Club v. Morton; Lujan v. Defenders of Wildlife.*

[5] *See Simon v. EKWRO.* In that case, the plaintiffs were injured by the refusal of private hospitals to provide free care. They claimed that this was caused by the IRS's lenient application of standards for hospitals to achieve tax-exempt charitable status. The Court found that the plaintiffs' inability to receive care was caused primarily by the actions of the hospital, not the government, and even if the IRS tightened up its standards, the hospitals might still refuse to provide care.

[6] In addition to *Lujan* cited in note 3 above, *see United States v. SCRAP* and *Simon v. EKWRO* for analysis of traceability or causation problems in standing.

[7] *See EKWRO* and *Lujan* for discussions of redressability.

[8] *See Data Processors; Air Courier Conference of America v. American Postal Workers Union.* The zone of interests test is an interpretation of APA §702, which grants standing to seek judicial review to parties "adversely affected or aggrieved within the meaning of a relevant statute." It may not apply in non-APA cases such as constitutional challenges to agency action.

[9] For example, a store owner injured cannot assert the rights of her customers to continue receiving food stamps even if the customers' loss of food stamps would injure the store owner by reducing her business. On the other hand, the store owner has standing to assert her own right to accept food stamps at the store.

[10] For example, health-care providers have been allowed to litigate their patients' rights to receive abortions on the ground that the patients may find it embarrassing to litigate, and also the patients' claims are transitory.

[11] The generalized grievance doctrine is founded on separation of powers concerns and holds that the political branches and not courts are the appropriate forum to resolve controversies that affect many people to a small degree where the plaintiff is not specially affected.

[12] In *SCRAP*, the Court stated that the fact that many people are injured by government action should not prevent standing. The plaintiffs in *SCRAP* were injured by increased litter and air and water pollution and only to a very small extent each. This decision seems to undercut the generalized grievance doctrine.

[13] The Court's paradigm case of a generalized grievance is a claim by taxpayers that they are injured when they have to pay taxes to support illegal government programs. However, the Court has allowed taxpayers to challenge subsidies to religion under the Establishment Clause. *See Flast v. Cohen.*

[14] In many statutes, especially recent environmental laws, Congress grants all persons or all citizens the right to challenge specified government action. These statutes override the prudential limits on standing and the zone of interests test. However, the plaintiffs must still establish that they meet the constitutional requirements for standing.

FIGURE 5

STANDARDS OF JUDICIAL REVIEW OF AGENCY ACTION

Use this chart to choose and apply the correct standard of review of agency action.

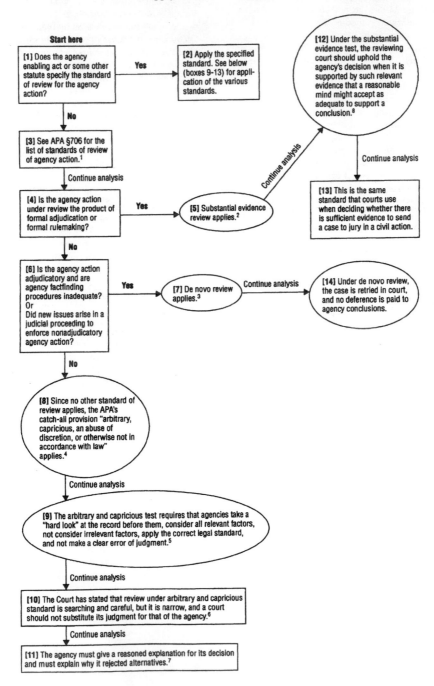

NOTES TO FIGURE 5
STANDARDS OF JUDICIAL REVIEW OF AGENCY ACTION

[1] This chart looks mainly at APA §706(2)(A), (E), and (F). Other subsections provide that agency action should be set aside if it violates constitutional rights (706(2)(B)), in excess of statutory jurisdiction (706(2)(C)) and without observance of proper procedure (706(2)(D)). Those sections are rarely applied, and they will not be addressed here.

[2] See APA §706(2)(D), specifying that the substantial evidence test applies in cases when the APA's formal adjudication provisions were applied or where agency action is "reviewed on the record of an agency hearing provided by statute." This final phrase is interpreted to denote formal procedures.

[3] The APA does not specify when de novo review applies, but the APA's legislative history clearly points toward application of the pre-APA understanding embodied in box 6 of the chart.

[4] APA 706(2)(A), which states the arbitrary and capricious test, contains no restriction on when it applies. Thus, it applies to all reviewable agency action. Because it is the most deferential standard of review in §706, those challenging agency action always prefer one of the other, less deferential, standards.

[5] *Citizens to Preserve Overton Park v. Volpe.*

[6] *Id.*

[7] *Id.*

[8] See *Universal Camera Corp. v. NLRB.*

FIGURE 6

JUDICIAL REVIEW OF AGENCY STATUTORY CONSTRUCTION: *CHEVRON*

Use this chart to choose and apply the correct standard of review of agency statutory construction under *Chevron*.[1]

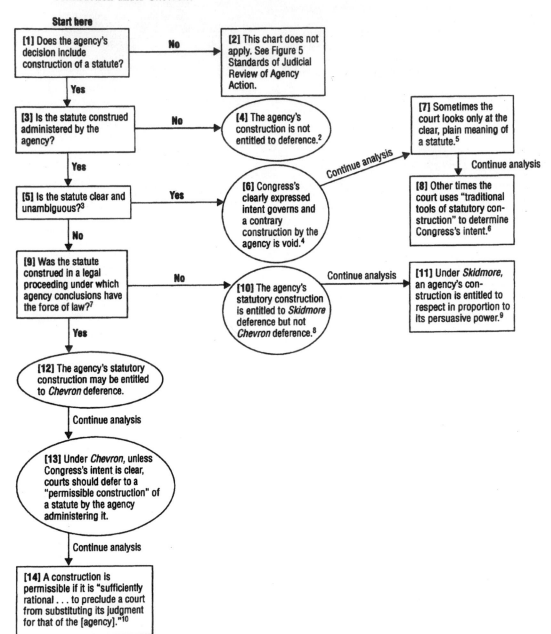

Start here

[1] Does the agency's decision include construction of a statute?

— **No** → [2] This chart does not apply. See Figure 5 Standards of Judicial Review of Agency Action.

Yes ↓

[3] Is the statute construed administered by the agency?

— **No** → [4] The agency's construction is not entitled to deference.[2]

Yes ↓

[5] Is the statute clear and unambiguous?[3]

— **Yes** → [6] Congress's clearly expressed intent governs and a contrary construction by the agency is void.[4]

Continue analysis → [7] Sometimes the court looks only at the clear, plain meaning of a statute.[5]

Continue analysis → [8] Other times the court uses "traditional tools of statutory construction" to determine Congress's intent.[6]

No ↓

[9] Was the statute construed in a legal proceeding under which agency conclusions have the force of law?[7]

— **No** → [10] The agency's statutory construction is entitled to *Skidmore* deference but not *Chevron* deference.[8]

Continue analysis → [11] Under *Skidmore*, an agency's construction is entitled to respect in proportion to its persuasive power.[9]

Yes ↓

[12] The agency's statutory construction may be entitled to *Chevron* deference.

Continue analysis ↓

[13] Under *Chevron*, unless Congress's intent is clear, courts should defer to a "permissible construction" of a statute by the agency administering it.

Continue analysis ↓

[14] A construction is permissible if it is "sufficiently rational . . . to preclude a court from substituting its judgment for that of the [agency]."[10]

NOTES TO FIGURE 6

JUDICIAL REVIEW OF AGENCY
STATUTORY CONSTRUCTION: *CHEVRON*

[1] This chart is concerned mainly with deference under *Chevron U.S.A. Inc. v. Natural Resources Defense Council, Inc.* Before *Chevron,* there were competing traditions regarding how much deference courts should give to agency statutory construction decisions. *Chevron* has largely displaced the older cases.

[2] Most agencies administer a particular statute or statutes. For example, the EPA administers the Clean Air Act and the Clean Water Act. Sometimes an agency must construe a statute other than the one it administers. The most common statute that would be involved in a case like this is the APA—agencies often must construe the APA to perform their procedural obligations properly. An agency's construction of the APA is never entitled to deference in court since no agency is charged with administration of the APA.

[3] This is *Chevron* step one, in which the Court looks for clear congressional intent. In *Chevron,* the Court stated that Congress's intent governed when Congress had "directly spoken to the precise question at issue." In subsequent cases, the Court has found congressional intent on a less demanding standard. See boxes 7-8 of this chart.

[4] Both agencies and courts are bound to follow Congress's intent in statutory construction.

[5] When it clearly expresses Congress's intent, the Court has refused to look beyond the clear, plain meaning of a statute. The Court even uses dictionaries to determine the plain meaning of statutory language. *See MCI Telecommunications Corp. v. American Telephone and Telegraph Co.* This is different from the original "directly spoken" standard because it does not require that the plain meaning address the precise issue; rather, the plain meaning points irresistibly to a particular answer to the question before the Court. For example, in the *MCI* case the issue was whether the FCC could allow certain phone companies to stop filing tariffs. The statute gave the FCC the power to modify the requirements of the statute, and the Court said that the plain meaning of "modify" did not include "eliminating" a requirement. Note that the statute did not address head-on whether the FCC could eliminate the tariff requirement.

[6] In *INS v. Cardoza-Fonseca,* the Court stated that courts should use "traditional tools of statutory interpretation" to discern Congress's intent in *Chevron* step one. This was viewed as a major limitation on *Chevron* since it would allow courts to refuse to defer to agencies in many more circumstances than would be the case if the "directly spoken" standard were applied. Traditional tools include canons of statutory construction, the structure of the statute, and even legislative history. The most notable application of this version of *Chevron* step one is the case in which the Court, looking mainly at other statutes and the structure of the food and drug laws, found that the FDA lacked authority to regulate the sale and promotion of tobacco products. *See FDA v. Brown and Williamson Tobacco Corp.*

[7] In some recent cases, the Court has distinguished between informal and formal expressions of agency views on the meaning of a statute. *See Mead Corp. v. United States; Christensen v. Harris County.* In more formal cases, such as rulemakings and formal adjudications, the agency has the power to issue rules with the force of law, and agency statutory interpretation may receive *Chevron* deference. In less formal cases, such as citations or opinion letters, the agency does not have the power to issue rules with the force of law, and statutory interpretations in such cases will not receive *Chevron* deference.

[8] *See Skidmore v. Swift Co.*

[9] Under *Skidmore,* courts defer to agency statutory interpretation when, based on all the circumstances, they find the agency's interpretation persuasive. While this is some deference, it is much less than under *Chevron* step two.

[10] *See Young v. Community Nutrition Institute.* This is a very deferential standard, basically applying the agency's interpretation unless it clearly is beyond the range of meaning the statute will bear.

FIGURE 7

CHOICE OF AGENCY PROCEDURE

Use this chart to determine whether an agency is required to use rulemaking or adjudication or has a choice.

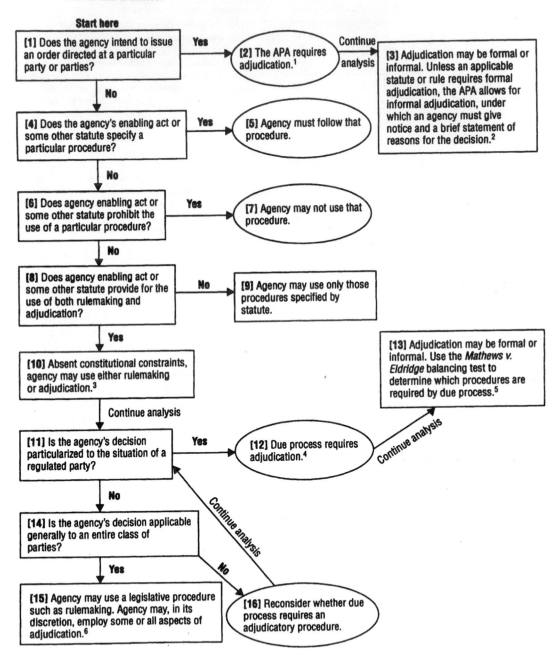

NOTES TO FIGURE 7

CHOICE OF AGENCY PROCEDURE

[1] 5 U.S.C. §551(7) defines "adjudication" as "agency process for the formulation of an order."

[2] See APA §555(e).

[3] Given a choice, agencies usually will choose a legislative procedure such as rulemaking because it is a simpler, less complex procedure. Courts also have recognized that rulemaking has certain policy advantages over adjudication, such as allowing more participation and more comprehensive decisionmaking, and because of these advantages, courts have liberally construed agency enabling acts and other statutes to allow agencies to use rulemaking.

[4] *See Londoner v. Denver.* Note that before due process applies, a party must have a protected interest, usually either liberty or property, at stake. When an agency is taking adverse action against a party, for example, by imposing a penalty or anti-pollution requirements, there is no question that property or liberty is at stake. However, in some cases, such as termination of government employment or government benefits, there may be a question whether liberty or property is present. For property to be involved, a statute, regulation, or entrenched understanding must provide standards against which government action is judged, such as a for-cause standard for termination of employment or a wealth test for benefits. *See Board of Regents v. Roth.* Liberty interests, on the other hand, are created by the Constitution itself. Freedom of movement, the ability to practice one's profession, and freedom from physical injury are among die liberties protected by the due process clauses from adverse government action.

[5] Even when due process under *Londoner* requires an adjudicatory hearing, formal adjudication is not necessarily required. Rather, the *Mathews v. Eldridge* balancing test is used to determine what procedures are required by due process. Under that test, the court considers the strength of the regulated party's interest, the likelihood that additional procedure will produce more accurate results, and the government's interest in minimizing process. When the regulated party's interests are relatively weak and existing procedures already produce a high degree of accuracy, due process may not require more than an informal adjudicatory procedure. On the other hand, when the regulated party's interests are relatively strong, such as the interest in subsistence welfare payments, and existing procedures produce a high likelihood of error, due process may require relatively formal procedures before the government can take even temporary adverse action. See also Flow Chart 9, Due Process and Adjudication.

[6] *See Bi-Metallic Investment Co. v. State Board of Equalization.*

FIGURE 8

INFORMAL RULEMAKING PROCEDURES

Use this chart to review the procedural requirements for "notice and comment" or informal rulemaking.

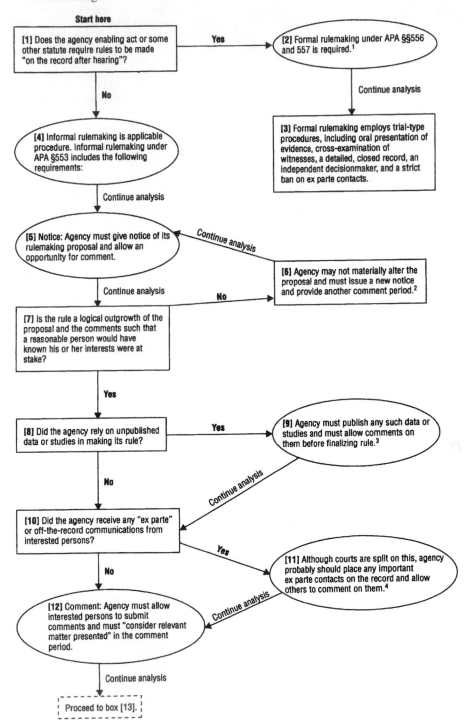

FIGURE 8 *(cont.)*

INFORMAL RULEMAKING PROCEDURES

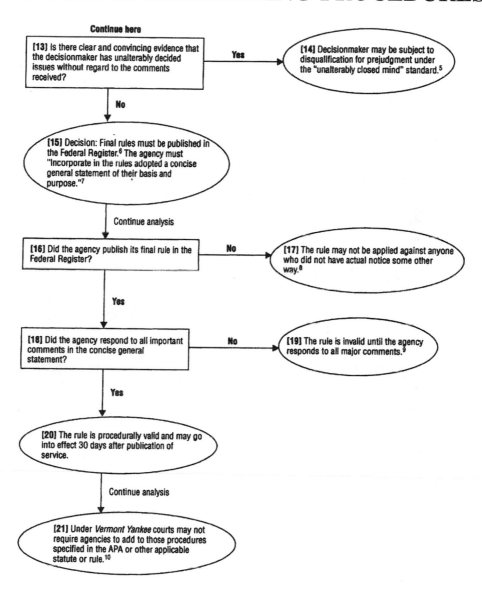

NOTES TO FIGURE 8
INFORMAL RULEMAKING PROCEDURES

[1] See APA §553(c), which states that "when rules are required by statute to be made on the record after opportunity for an agency hearing, sections 556 and 557 of this title apply instead of this subsection." Sections 556 and 557 contain formal adjudicatory procedures. Because formal rulemaking is expensive and time-consuming, agencies rarely use it, and courts do not require agencies to use it unless a statute clearly requires it.

[2] APA §553(b)(3) requires notice of the "terms or substance of the proposed rule or a description of the subjects and issues involved." When the final rule differs significantly from the original proposal, there is a possibility that affected parties may not have realized that their interests were at stake in the rulemaking and might not have submitted comments to protect their interests. In light of this potential problem, courts have held that agencies may not make material alterations in the proposal without conducting a second round of notice and comment on the new proposal. The standard has also been stated as the "logical outgrowth" test — final rules must be the logical outgrowth of the original proposal and the comments received. The basic principle is the same — all affected parties must be on notice that their interests are at stake so that they have a reasonable opportunity to submit comments.

[3] *See United States v. Nova Scotia Food Prods. Corp.*

[4] No provision of the APA prohibits ex parte communication in informal rulemaking. However, some courts have held that ex parte communications violate §553 because they sidestep the public comment process, create a secret record, and deprive others of an adequate opportunity to comment. While some courts have stated that agencies should refuse to receive ex parte comments, others have been less strict and require only that agencies place all important ex parte comments on the public rulemaking record.

[5] *See Association of National Advertisers v. FTC.* The APA does not address prejudgment in rulemaking, and perhaps because of this, courts rarely if ever disqualify a decisionmaker under this standard. This standard is much less demanding than the standard for prejudgment in adjudication, where the appearance that the decisionmaker has in some measure prejudged the facts or law of an adjudicatory dispute can result in disqualification.

[6] APA §552(a)(1)(D).

[7] APA §553 (c).

[8] APA §552(a). *See also Morton v. Ruiz.* A party with actual notice of the rule cannot complain that the rule was not published in the Federal Register. Thus, where rules affect a small number of parties, the agency may personally serve parties with copies of the rule.

[9] *See United States v. Nova Scotia Food Prods. Corp.*

[10] Some courts had held that for complicated rules, agencies must employ procedures in addition to those specified in the APA or other applicable statutes or rules. The Supreme Court, in the *Vermont Yankee* case, rejected all such holdings and stated emphatically that, absent unconstitutionality, courts have no authority to require agencies to employ procedures other than those required by statute or rule.

FIGURE 9

DUE PROCESS AND ADJUDICATION

Use this chart to determine when due process requires adjudication and, of so, how much process is due before government takes adverse action.

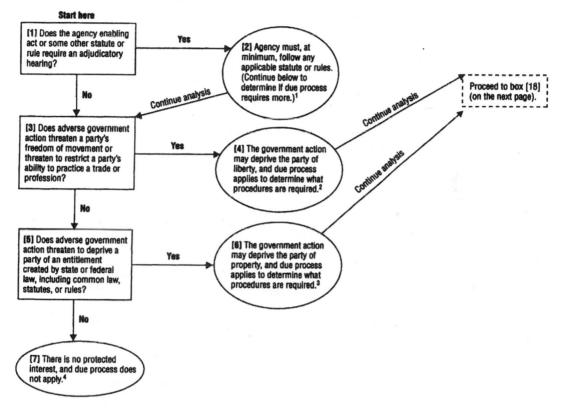

continues on next page   *See footnotes after final page of chart*

FIGURE 9 (*cont.*)

DUE PROCESS AND ADJUDICATION

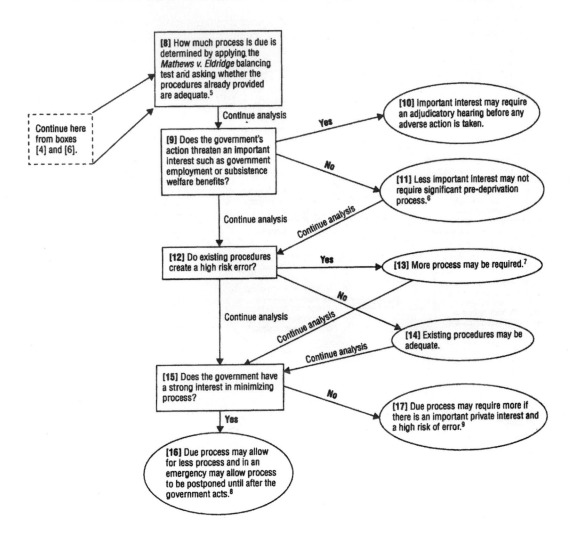

NOTES TO FIGURE 9

DUE PROCESS AND ADJUDICATION

[1] Agencies must provide whatever process is required by applicable statutes and rules. However, it should be noted that courts, for policy reasons, construe statutes, whenever possible, to maximize agency flexibility and thus do not favor construing statutes to require agencies to conduct formal adjudicatory hearings. It is extremely unlikely that due process will ever require more process than a full adjudicatory hearing under APA §§554, 556, and 557.

[2] Liberty interests are created by the Constitution and include such basic rights as the right to freedom from restraint, the right to bodily integrity, and the right to engage in a chosen occupation. Such interests may be restricted by government, but only pursuant to procedures that comport with due process.

[3] Property interests are not created by the Constitution but rather are created by an external source of law such as a statute, a rule of common law, or a recognized government practice. The basic test for the existence of property is whether some source of law creates a legitimate claim of entitlement rather than a unilateral expectation. A legitimate claim of entitlement exists when there are legally prescribed criteria for evaluating the propriety of government action, such as a for-cause requirement for termination of government employment. When government action is purely discretionary, such as at-will government employment, there is no entitlement and thus no property interest.

[4] Interests in life are not addressed here as they are rarely at issue in administrative law.

[5] The *Mathews v. Eldridge* balancing test governs how much process is due when government action threatens to deprive a party of a protected interest. Existing procedures are used as a baseline, and the test is used to determine whether due process requires more. Under that test, the court considers the strength of the regulated party's interest, the likelihood that additional procedure will produce more accurate results, and the government's interest in minimizing process. When the regulated party's interests are relatively weak and existing procedures already produce a high degree of accuracy, due

process may not require more than what is already provided. On the other hand, when the regulated party's interests are relatively strong, such as the interest in subsistence welfare payments, and existing procedures produce a high likelihood of error, due process may require relatively formal procedures before government can take even temporary adverse action. The test is not precise, and each factor simply nudges the decision in one direction or another.

[6] Claimants often seek a pre-deprivation adjudicatory hearing, while government prefers to postpone the hearing until after it takes action. The Supreme Court has required pre-deprivation hearings when welfare benefits and government employment are at stake but has not required much in the way of pre-deprivation process in other situations, such as the termination of disability benefits, which are not based on the wealth of the recipient.

[7] Typically, courts would add requirements such as an oral hearing, confrontation and cross-examination of adverse witnesses, a closed record (no ex parte contacts or non-record evidence), and an impartial decisionmaker. Regarding the impartial decisionmaker, the decisionmaker may not have a significant pecuniary or other interest in the outcome of the case and may not have expressed views indicating prejudgment. Bias and prejudgment raise a substantial likelihood of an erroneous decision.

[8] Where it is impractical for government to hold an advance hearing or where an emergency exists, such as contaminated or adulterated food, the Court has allowed virtually all process to be postponed until after the adverse action has already been taken. Also, in *Mathews v. Eldridge* itself, the Court noted that the unlikelihood that the government would be able to recoup disability payments made in error militated in favor of postponing the hearing until after benefits had been suspended.

[9] It's not that the lack of a government interest in minimizing process strengthens a claim for more process, it's that, all other things being equal, the lack of such a government interest means that it is more likely that a court would require more process.

FIGURE 10

INFORMATION GATHERING AND INSPECTIONS

Use this chart to analyze whether an agency may gather information or conduct an inspection.

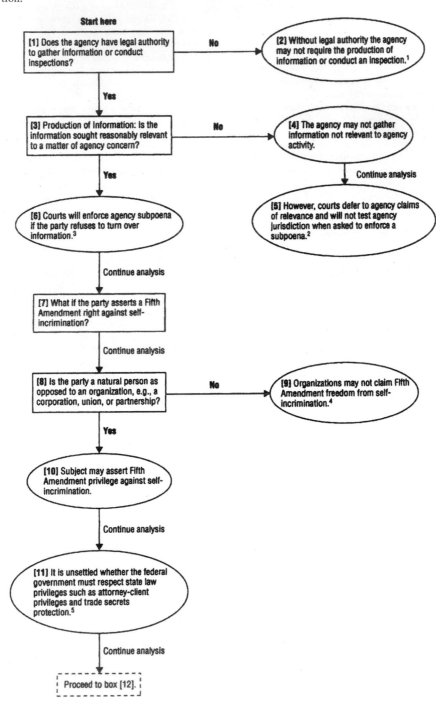

FIGURE 10 (*cont.*)

INFORMATION GATHERING AND INSPECTIONS

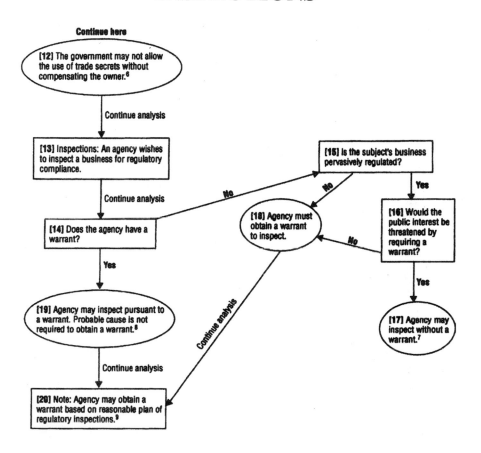

<small>NOTES TO FIGURE 10</small>
INFORMATION GATHERING AND INSPECTIONS

[1] APA §555(c).

[2] *See United States v. Morton Salt Co.*

[3] *See United States v. Sturm, Ruger & Co.*

[4] *See Bellis v. United States* (partner in a small law firm has no Fifth Amendment right to withhold partnership records). The Court has held that a natural person who is the custodian of business records may not assert a Fifth Amendment right against turning over business records even if the existence of the records would incriminate the person. *See Braswell v. United States.*

[5] In *EEOC v. University of Pennsylvania*, the court upheld and order to turn over university records even if state law might have recognized a privilege based on academic freedom.

[6] *See Ruckelshaus v. Monsanto Co.*

[7] *See Donovan v. Dewey; New York v. Burger.*

[8] *See Marshall v. Barlow's Inc.*

[9] *Id.*

FIGURE 11

FEDERAL TORT CLAIMS

Use this chart to analyze the liability of the federal government and federal officials for tortious conduct.

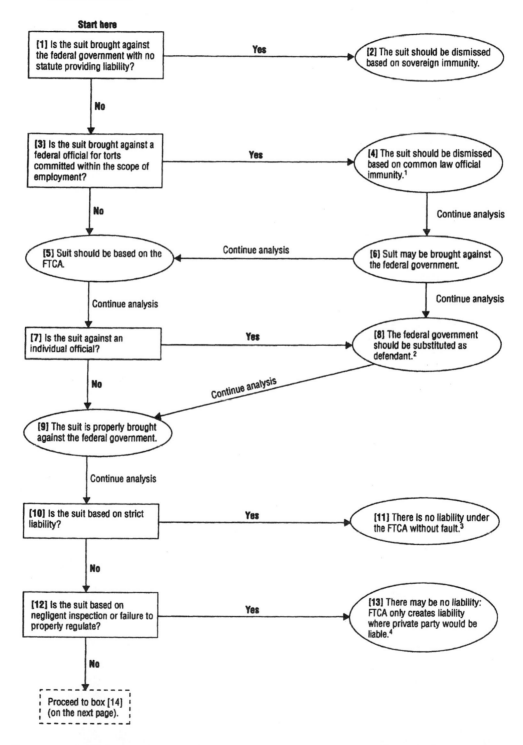

FIGURE 11 (*cont.*)

FEDERAL TORT CLAIMS

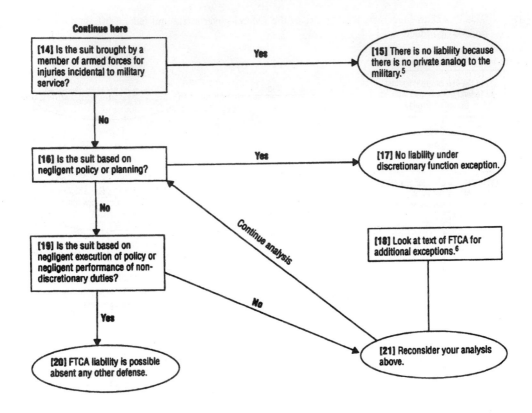

NOTES TO FIGURE 11

FEDERAL TORT CLAIMS

[1] *Barr v. Matteo.*

[2] Under the Federal Tort Claims Act (FTCA), any tort suit against an individual federal official should be dismissed and the federal government should be substituted as defendant. The official is not liable even if it turns out that the federal government has a good defense in the particular case. The FTCA, in effect, displaces all other tort- based liability against federal officials.

[3] The FTCA creates federal government liability for a "negligent or wrongful act or omission." This language has been interpreted to bar liability without fault, such as strict liability. *See Laird v. Nelms.*

[4] The FTCA provides for liability "in the same manner and to the same extent as a private individual under like circumstances." This language has been interpreted to mean that there is no liability for conduct normally engaged in only by government because there is no analogous private liability.

[5] This goes beyond injuries while engaged in actual military actions such as battle. For example, the analysis applies to medical malpractice actions brought against military doctors treating members of the armed services at military hospitals in peacetime. *See Feres v. United States.* The *Feres* doctrine has been criticized for going beyond the FTCA exception for claims arising out of "combatant activities of the military ... during time of war." It is questionable whether the courts should expand the statutory exception.

[6] The FTCA has numerous exceptions from liability, including claims arising out of losses arising out of postal service errors, claims arising out of the administration of taxes, claims arising out of fiscal operations of the Treasury, claims arising in foreign countries, and more. The most important exception is the discretionary function exception because it covers a broad range of conduct across the entire spectrum of government activity.

FIGURE 12

CONSTITUTIONAL DAMAGES LIABILITY OF FEDERAL OFFICIALS

Use this chart to determine whether an individual federal official may be liable for damages for constitutional violations. Assume the Constitution has been violated and the plaintiff has been injured.

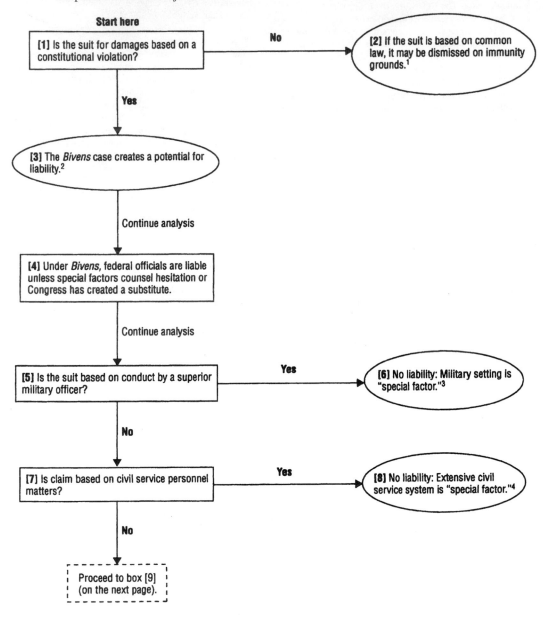

Start here

[1] Is the suit for damages based on a constitutional violation?

No → **[2]** If the suit is based on common law, it may be dismissed on immunity grounds.[1]

Yes ↓

[3] The *Bivens* case creates a potential for liability.[2]

Continue analysis ↓

[4] Under *Bivens*, federal officials are liable unless special factors counsel hesitation or Congress has created a substitute.

Continue analysis ↓

[5] Is the suit based on conduct by a superior military officer?

Yes → **[6]** No liability: Military setting is "special factor."[3]

No ↓

[7] Is claim based on civil service personnel matters?

Yes → **[8]** No liability: Extensive civil service system is "special factor."[4]

No ↓

Proceed to box [9] (on the next page).

FIGURE 12 (*cont.*)

CONSTITUTIONAL DAMAGES LIABILITY OF FEDERAL OFFICIALS

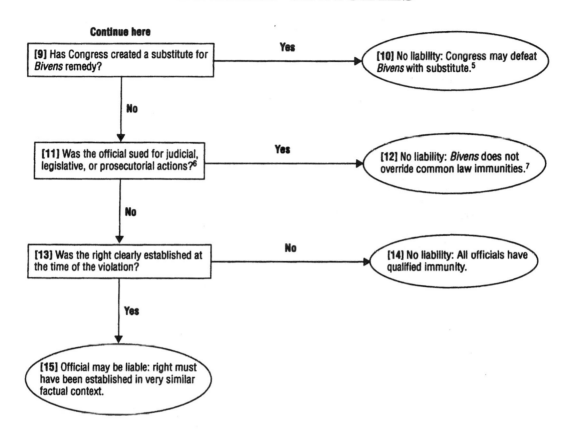

NOTES TO FIGURE 12

CONSTITUTIONAL DAMAGES LIABILITY OF FEDERAL OFFICIALS

[1] *Barr v. Matteo* holds that federal officials may assert immunity from suit for damages based on common law. The Federal Tort Claims Act provides that when a federal official is sued for damages based on common law-type claims, the federal government is substituted as defendant and the official is not liable even if the federal government turns out also to be not liable.

[2] *Bivens v. Six Unknown Named Agents of Federal Bureau of Narcotics.*

[3] *Chappell v. Wallace.*

[4] *Bush v. Lucas.*

[5] It is not sufficient that a parallel remedy is available. Rather, Congress must designate that the alternative remedy is a substitute for the *Bivens* remedy. *See Carlson v. Green,* in which the *Bivens* remedy was allowed to coexist with a remedy against the government under the Federal Tort Claims Act. However, in some cases, the existence of a parallel remedy has contributed to a finding of "special factors counseling hesitation" without a declaration that the *Bivens* remedy has been displaced. *See, e.g., Bush v. Lucas.*

[6] The *Bivens* action does not override traditional common law immunities which held that judges, legislators, and prosecutors were absolutely immune from damages liability. The Supreme Court applies a functional approach to determine when an official is shielded by absolute immunity. Administrative officials performing judicial, legislative, and prosecutorial functions are also absolutely immune. However, absolute immunity does not extend to functions other than those for which the immunity exists, For example, a judge is absolutely immune from damages for judicial decisions but is not absolutely immune from claims arising out of administrative actions such as hiring and firing court personnel.

[7] The same immunities apply in cases brought against state and local officials under 42 U.S.C. §1983.

FIGURE 13

FREEDOM OF INFORMATION

Use this chart to analyze issues regarding the requirements of the Freedom of Information Act (FOIA).

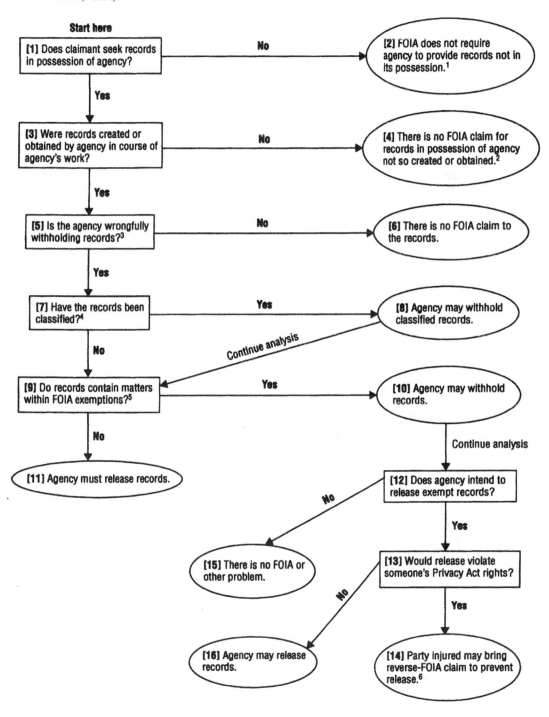

NOTES TO FIGURE 13
FREEDOM OF INFORMATION

[1] *Kissinger v. Reporters Committee for Freedom of the Press.* FOIA creates liability only when records are "wrongfully withheld." Records are not wrongfully withheld if they are not in the agency's possession.

[2] For example, FOIA does not require an agency to turn over documents that an official keeps in an agency office if the documents were not created or obtained as part of agency activities.

[3] "Wrongfully withholding" means simply that the agency is not providing them when FOIA requires it to. See also footnote 1 to this chart.

[4] FOIA contains an exception for records that have been classified under an executive order "to be kept secret in the interest of national defense or foreign policy." The records must have been actually so classified, not merely classifiable.

[5] FOIA contains a long list of exemptions from disclosure, including personnel matters, trade secrets, records compiled for law enforcement purposes, records regarding regulation of financial institutions, and geological information. If records contain some exempt material along with material that is not exempt, the agency must disclose the non-exempt material if it can be segregated from the exempt material.

[6] The Privacy Act prohibits agencies from disclosing records concerning an individual without that individual's consent. It does not, however, prohibit disclosure of records that would otherwise be subject to disclosure under FOIA. The Court has recognized a claim under FOIA, known as revcrse-FOIA, to prevent an agency from disclosing records that are not required by FOIA to be disclosed and would violate an individual's privacy interests.

CAPSULE SUMMARY

CAPSULE SUMMARY

SUMMARY OF CONTENTS

Capsule Summary

CHAPTER 1

ADMINISTRATIVE LAW FUNDAMENTALS

I. OVERVIEW OF ADMINISTRATIVE LAW

Administrative law regulates the exercise of authority by executive officials including officials of independent agencies.

A. Administrative Law Derives Mainly From Four Sources

1. The Constitution

2. The Administrative Procedure Act

3. Particular agency enabling acts

4. Administrative common law

B. The Study of Administrative Law

In studying administrative law, the focus is on the source and limits of agency power, potential constitutional limitations on agency power, and the procedural requirements placed on the agency by the Constitution, the APA, the agency's enabling act, and any other administrative law doctrine.

C. Judicial Review

Judicial review is the mechanism for enforcing procedural and substantive constraints on agency action. Thus, it is vital to be aware of whether judicial review is available, and if so, what standard of judicial review governs.

D. Enforcement

Regulatory norms are enforceable by agencies and sometimes also by private parties affected by alleged violations of regulatory norms. It is important to be aware of the enforcement tools available to both sets of potential enforcers.

II. THE ORIGINS AND ROLES OF ADMINISTRATIVE AGENCIES

The administrative state, as we know it, began in 1887 with the creation of the Interstate Commerce Commission, although the antecedents to the administrative state go back to the beginning of the republic.

A. **Structure of the Administrative State**

While most federal administrative agencies are within a department of the executive branch, Congress has designated some agencies as "independent" — not within any department of the federal government and not under the supervision of the President or any cabinet officer.

B. **The Roles of Administrative Agencies**

Administrative agencies, as the name implies, administer government programs established by Congress.

III. THE FUNCTIONS OF ADMINISTRATIVE AGENCIES

Administrative agencies perform a wide variety of functions in the United States at the local, state, and federal levels. These functions include distribution of government benefits, granting of licenses and permits, and policymaking in a wide variety of regulated areas. Agencies employ a wide array of policymaking methods including rulemaking, adjudication, and informal policymaking.

IV. PUBLIC INTEREST AND PUBLIC CHOICE UNDERSTANDINGS OF ADMINISTRATIVE LAW

Public interest theory explains administrative policymaking and the structure of administrative agencies based on the traditional notion that agencies act to further the public good and are structured to maximize their ability to further the public good. Public choice theory, by contrast, explains regulation and the structure of agencies as products of the political process in which parties with political power enlist government coercion to achieve goals that they could not achieve in a free market. Public choice theory explains agency structure as maximizing the ability of parties with power to influence government action, rather than as structures created because of views about good policy.

CHAPTER 2

SEPARATION OF POWERS AND DISTRIBUTION OF ADMINISTRATIVE POWER

I. THE NONDELEGATION DOCTRINE

The nondelegation doctrine prohibits Congress from delegating excessive legislative discretion to the executive branch.

A. Historical Origins of the Nondelegation Doctrine

Early cases stated that the Constitution absolutely prohibited the delegation of legislative authority from Congress to the executive branch. Delegations of discretionary authority to the executive branch were permissible so long as Congress made the legislative decisions and the executive branch merely "filled up the details." The discretion exercised by executive officials was not legislative but rather was discretion inherent in execution of the laws.

B. The Intelligible Principle Test

In *J.W. Hampton, Jr. & Co. v. United States,* 276 U.S. 394 (1928), the Court stated that a delegation is permissible when Congress "lay down by legislative act an intelligible principle to which the person or body authorized to fix such rates is directed to conform." The "intelligible principle" standard remains the test for determining whether Congress has delegated too much legislative discretion to the executive branch.

C. Delegation During the New Deal

The Supreme Court greeted New Deal legislation with a great deal of skepticism, and in addition to many decisions invalidating state and federal legislation on other grounds, it struck down three federal statutory provisions on two nondelegation grounds. First, the legislation granted broad enforcement powers without specifying when enforcement was required. *See Panama Refining Co. v. Ryan,* 293 U.S. 388 (1935). Second, power was sometimes delegated to private groups, such as trade associations. *See Carter v. Carter Coal Co.,* 298 U.S. 238 (1936). Each of these features was held unconstitutional.

D. The Return to a Lenient Nondelegation Doctrine

Beginning in the 1940s and continuing to the present time, the Court has been very lenient in nondelegation cases, requiring only a minimally intelligible principle for a statute to withstand nondelegation attack. Even though the Court continues to evaluate challenges to delegations on the "intelligible principle" standard, the Court always manages to find sufficient legislative guidance to withstand attack, even in very general legislative instructions and goals.

E. *Benzene* and Nondelegation

A recent hint of a strict nondelegation doctrine was in the *Benzene* case, in which both the plurality and concurring opinions argued that standardless prosecutorial discretion under the Occupational Safety and Health Act (OSH Act) created nondelegation problems. *See Industrial Union Department, AFL-CIO v. American Petroleum Institute (The Benzene Cases),* 448 U.S. 607 (1980). Justice Stevens's plurality opinion relied upon the nondelegation doctrine to limit the Occupational Safety and Health Administration's (OSHA) authority to prescribe occupational health and safety standards to situations in which a substantial health or safety risk has rendered a workplace "unsafe." Justice Rehnquist's *Benzene* concurrence went further, arguing that the statute violated the nondelegation doctrine because it failed to specify when the agency was required to pursue the goal of a virtually risk-free workplace. Justice Rehnquist's opinion argued that the Court should reinvigorate the nondelegation doctrine because it serves the three related goals of (1) forcing Congress, the representative branch of government, to make important policy choices; (2) increasing the guidance under which agencies act; and (3) facilitating judicial review by requiring more definite statutory standards against which courts can measure administrative decisions.

F. **Attempted Revival of the Nondelegation Doctrine:** *Whitman v. American Trucking Associations, Inc.*

Since the *Benzene* case, the Court has rejected several delegation challenges. In *American Trucking Associations, Inc. v. U.S. Environmental Protection Agency,* 175 F.3d 1027 (D.C. Cir. 1999), the D.C. Circuit found a violation of the nondelegation doctrine not so much because the statute lacked an intelligible principle but rather because EPA had not adopted an intelligible principle to confine its own discretion. The Supreme Court reversed, reaffirming the intelligible principle test and rejecting the idea that an agency can cure a delegation violation with its own limiting construction. The Court observed that under the D.C. Circuit's analysis, leaving it to the agency to decide on a limiting construction should itself be a nondelegation violation. *See Whitman v. American Trucking Associations, Inc.,* 531 U.S. 457 (2001).

II. CONGRESSIONAL CONTROL OF ADMINISTRATIVE AGENCIES

A. **Congressional Influence**

Members of Congress attempt to influence agencies through formal and informal means. These include numerous informal contacts, influence over appointments to agencies, and, more formally, controlling agency funding, statutorily restricting agency action, and statutorily overruling regulations. Congress also attempts to increase its influence on agency action by creating independent agencies that are less subject to presidential control.

B. **The Legislative Veto and Review of Regulations**

Until the Supreme Court held it unconstitutional, the legislative veto was an important device used by Congress to control agency action. Under legislative veto provisions of many enabling acts, Congress could, without presentment to the President, reject agency action (usually regulations). This could be done, depending on the particular provision, by a vote of both houses of Congress, by one house of Congress, or in some cases, even by a single congressional committee. In *Immigration and Naturalization Service v. Chadha,* 462 U.S. 919 (1983), the Supreme Court held a one-house legislative veto unconstitutional on the grounds that the one-house veto violated the bicameralism and presentment requirements of the Constitution. Bicameralism and presentment apply to all congressional actions that affect the legal rights and duties of persons outside the legislative branch. Two-house vetoes are also unconstitutional because they violate the requirement that legislation be presented to the President.

C. **Congressional Involvement in Appointment and Removal of Executive Officials**

1. **Appointments:** The Appointments Clause of the Constitution provides for presidential appointment, with Senate confirmation, of officers of the United States. The clause allows Congress to specify that inferior officers may be appointed by the President alone, by heads of departments, or the courts of

law. In *Buckley v. Valeo,* 424 U.S. 1 (1975), the Court held that officials appointed under a procedure not provided for in the Appointments Clause may not exercise authority under the laws of the United States. Congress, especially the Senate through its advice and consent power, exercises significant political influence over presidential appointments.

2. **Removal:** Officers of the United States may not be subject to removal by congressional action, except by impeachment by the House and conviction by the Senate. Congress statutorily restricts the removal of administrative officials and Congress may delegate the removal power to an official under presidential control. For example, in *Morrison v. Olson,* 487 U.S. 654 (1988), the Court upheld the Independent Counsel Act under which a prosecutor appointed to investigate alleged wrongdoing by executive officials could be removed only by the Attorney General, and only for cause.

3. **Members of Congress may not serve as administrative officials:** The Incompatibility Clause, Article I, Section 6, Clause 2 of the Constitution, forbids members of Congress from holding an executive appointment during their term in Congress. In addition to violating the Incompatibility Clause, it would violate separation of powers for members of Congress to serve as administrators.

III. EXECUTIVE CONTROL OF ADMINISTRATIVE AGENCIES

A. Inherent Executive Power

In *Youngstown Sheet & Tube Co. v. Sawyer,* 343 U.S. 579 (1953), the Supreme Court held that President Truman lacked inherent power, without congressional authorization, to order seizure of the nation's steel mills when they were threatened with a strike during the Korean War. In a famous concurring opinion, Justice Jackson argued that the President's power is at its greatest when acting pursuant to express or implied congressional authorization and at its weakest when acting contrary to Congress's will. Jackson argued that when the President acts with neither support nor disapproval from Congress, the President's power to act may be concurrent with Congress's, and the lack of congressional authorization does not necessarily mean that the President is going beyond executive authority.

B. The Unitary Executive Theory

The unitary executive theory holds that the Constitution vests all executive power in the President, and thus any attempt by Congress to insulate officials and agencies from complete presidential control is suspect and probably unconstitutional.

C. Presidential Appointment and Removal of Executive Officials

1. **Appointment:** The President, with the advice and consent of the Senate, appoints officers of the United States. Congress may specify that inferior officers are appointed by the President alone, by the heads of departments, or by the courts of law.

a. Principal officers: While there is no clear line between principal officers and inferior officers, principal officers are high-level officials in the executive branch, such as department heads and heads of independent agencies.

b. Inferior officers: Inferior officers are lower-level executive officials who are under the supervision of other executive officials beneath the President. In *Morrison v. Olson,* the Court held that an independent counsel investigating wrongdoing by executive branch officials was an inferior officer because of the limited scope and duration of the independent prosecutor's appointment and the Attorney General's removal power.

c. Employees: Employees are low level officials who are employed by the federal government but exercise no discretion or authority to administer federal law. They are neither principal nor inferior officers and thus may be appointed pursuant to procedures other than those provided for in the appointments clause, such as a civil-service-type appointments process.

2. **Removal:** The Constitution does not mention the removal of officials except through impeachment and conviction. In the absence of statutory restrictions, the President has the power to remove executive officials at will. Congress may, under most circumstances, restrict the President's power to remove executive officials, but Congress itself may not retain advice and consent power over removal of officials or participate in the removal of officials except through impeachment.

D. Direct Presidential Supervision of Administrative Agencies

The degree to which the President has inherent authority to supervise administrative agencies is an unsettled and controversial area of law. Today, all but the highest government positions are filled with civil service employees with statutory job security. Further, the First Amendment limits the President's right to replace government officials for political reasons.

E. The Line Item Veto

The Line Item Veto Act is unconstitutional since in effect it grants the President unilateral power to amend or repeal legislation. *See Clinton v. City of New York,* 524 U.S. 417 (1998). The Act gave the President the power to cancel items in bills after signing the bills. The problem with this is that once the President signed the bill passed by Congress, the entire bill became law, and only further legislation by both Houses of Congress could amend or repeal it.

IV. ADJUDICATION WITHIN ADMINISTRATIVE AGENCIES

Agency adjudication raises a separation of powers problem because Article III vests the judicial power of the United States in the Article III courts, and it has been argued that administrative agencies usurp that power when they adjudicate cases. However, the Supreme Court has approved of a great deal of agency adjudication as long as administrative agencies adjudicate in areas closely connected to federal regulatory programs and do not seize the central attributes of judicial power. Limited jurisdiction, limited powers, and judicial review and enforcement of judgments in Article III courts are factors that support the constitutionality of administrative adjudication.

CHAPTER 3

THE AVAILABILITY OF JUDICIAL REVIEW OF ADMINISTRATIVE DECISIONS

I. JURISDICTION

The petition for judicial review must be brought in a court that has jurisdiction over the claim, normally either the district court or the court of appeals. In most cases, the choice between the court of appeals and the district court is simple because the agency's governing statute identifies the proper forum for judicial review. Most of these statutes provide for review of administrative action in the court of appeals. If no statute states otherwise, review must be sought in the district court under that court's original jurisdiction. For reasons of judicial economy, courts interpret specific statutes, whenever possible, to direct review to the court of appeals — even in cases of informal agency action where there is no formal agency record.

II. REVIEWABILITY

A. Presumption in Favor of Judicial Review

There is a longstanding presumption that judicial review of agency action is available. The Administrative Procedure Act (APA) provisions granting judicial review in favor of persons adversely affected or aggrieved by final agency action reinforce this presumption, subject to APA created exceptions.

B. Exceptions to Reviewability

APA §701 specifies two situations in which APA judicial review is not available: when "statutes preclude judicial review," §701(a)(1), and when "agency action is committed to agency discretion by law." §701(a)(2).

1. **Agency action:** Review under the APA is available only for agency action. The President is not an agency within the meaning of the APA. Further, the Supreme Court has required that the petitioner identify a particular agency action that is being challenged, holding that APA review is not available to challenge the general manner in which an agency regulates. *See Norton v. Southern Utah Wilderness Alliance*, 542 U.S. 55 (2004).

2. **Statutory preclusion:** For a statute to preclude judicial review it should explicitly mention judicial review and either preclude it completely or provide for a particular form of judicial review and preclude all others.

3. **"Committed to agency discretion by law":** The traditional understanding of "committed to agency discretion by law" is that judicial review is not available when the governing statutes are drawn in such broad terms that in a given case there is no law to apply. Review may also be "committed to agency discretion by law" when the statute suggests that Congress intended for the agency to have final authority over a decision or when the agency action is in a category of

administrative decisions that have traditionally been held to be committed to agency discretion.

4. **Reviewability of prosecutorial discretion:** The Supreme Court has created, under APA §701(a)(2), a strong presumption that agency prosecutorial decisions, such as choosing targets for administrative enforcement or areas in which to regulate, are unreviewable as "committed to agency discretion by law." The presumption exists because few enabling acts contain precise instructions about when an agency must act, and because the decision of when to act and against whom often involves balancing multiple factors such as available resources and effective enforcement policy. The presumption against review of prosecutorial discretion may be rebutted if the agency's enabling act requires the agency to act under certain specified circumstances or within a certain time period.

C. Preclusion of Review of Constitutional Questions

Because precluding judicial review of constitutional challenges itself raises a serious constitutional question, courts have interpreted statutes precluding judicial review to preclude review only of nonconstitutional questions, while preserving review of constitutional issues. It is unsettled whether and to what degree Congress may bar review of constitutional questions.

III. STANDING TO SECURE JUDICIAL REVIEW

A party seeking judicial review must have standing. Constitutional standing doctrine requires that the plaintiff must be injured by the challenged conduct and must stand to gain from a favorable ruling (redressability). In addition to the constitutional injury and redressability requirements, the federal courts have imposed prudential standing limitations that bar plaintiffs from asserting the rights of third parties and from seeking redress for generalized grievances, which affect society as a whole.

There are exceptions to the prudential limitations such as the doctrine that allows third parties to assert the constitutional rights of those who are unable to assert their own rights. The party asserting the rights must still meet the constitutional injury and redressability requirements. Further, because the prudential limitations on standing are judge made and not constitutionally compelled, Congress has the power to overrule them.

A. Standing: The Old "Legal Right" Test

Early administrative law standing cases allowed review only on behalf of parties whose own legal rights had been allegedly violated by agency action. Parties injured by agency treatment of others, for example, when an agency loosens regulation on a competitor, lacked standing to seek judicial review of the agency's treatment of the third party or parties.

B. Standing: The "Injury-in-Fact Fairly Traceable" Test

In reaction to criticism of the legal right test, the Court has replaced it with the requirement that the plaintiff have suffered an injury-in-fact that is fairly traceable to the challenged conduct and is redressable by a favorable judgment. Further, the plaintiff must be in the zone of interests of the statute under which relief is sought.

1. **Abstract injury not sufficient:** Persons or groups with an abstract interest in a regulatory scheme do not have standing without an actual injury. For example, an environmental group does not have standing to challenge the treatment of a wilderness area unless members of the group actually use the area in question.

2. **The injury must be "fairly traceable" to the challenged conduct:** The injury must be "fairly traceable" to the challenged conduct, or in other words, the conduct challenged must have actually caused the injury. While the concept of causation is not particularly difficult to understand, it is often not clear why the Supreme Court finds causation present in some cases and absent in others.

3. **Redressability:** To have standing, the plaintiff must show that the remedy sought will redress the injury. A plaintiff seeking relief against past harm may lack standing on redressability grounds if the harm is not continuing and the plaintiff is not entitled to damages or any other form of compensation for the past harm.

C. APA Standing and the Zone of Interests Test

The Supreme Court has held that to have standing the plaintiff must establish that "the interest sought to be protected by the complainant is arguably within the zone of interests to be protected or regulated by the statute or constitutional guarantee in question." The zone of interests test applies to cases in which the plaintiff seeks to challenge agency treatment of someone else (such as a competitor) and asks whether the plaintif's interests were considered by Congress or the regulatory body in the decision to regulate the third party.

D. Associational Standing

Associations (such as interest groups and trade associations) have standing to litigate their own claims and also the claims of their members as long as the members themselves would have standing to sue, the interests the association is suing over are within the association's purpose, and the litigation will not be adversely affected by the absence of individual plaintiffs.

IV. THE TIMING OF JUDICIAL REVIEW: RIPENESS, EXHAUSTION, AND MOOTNESS

Judicial review may not be sought too early (ripeness), too late (mootness), and in some cases, without exhausting administrative remedies.

A. Ripeness and the APA's Grant of Review of "Final Agency Action"

APA §704's grants of judicial review of "final agency action for which there is no other adequate remedy in a court" is essentially a ripeness requirement, which excludes from review agency action that is not yet complete. Even though a rule is "final" upon promulgation, the Supreme Court has held that a rule is ripe for review upon promulgation (before enforcement) only if the issues are fit for judicial review and the party seeking review would suffer substantial hardship if review were delayed until after enforcement. *Abbott Labs, et al. v. Gardner,* 387 U.S. 136, 148 (1967).

B. Ripeness of Informal Agency Action

When informal agency action has the effect of granting or denying permission to take a requested course of action, a court might consider it final agency action even though the decision was made without any formal procedures.

C. Ripeness of Agency Inaction or Refusal to Act

If the agency formally declines to take action, that decision can be a "final agency action" subject to judicial review. If an agency fails to answer a request to act, the failure to act is ripe for review only in the rare circumstance that agency inaction is the equivalent of a decision not to act or appears from the circumstances to amount to a decision not to act. If an agency is statutorily required to act in an emergency, agency inaction in response to a petition alleging an emergency may amount to a decision that no emergency exists that requires agency action.

D. Exhaustion of Administrative Remedies Prior to Seeking Judicial Review

One of the oldest, most established doctrines in administrative law is that challengers must exhaust remedies within the agency before seeking judicial review.

  1. Exceptions to the exhaustion requirement: A party is not required to exhaust administrative remedies when (1) exhaustion would cause undue prejudice to the protection of the rights at issue; (2) the administrative agency lacks power to grant effective relief; or (3) the exhaustion would be futile because the administrative body is biased.

  2. APA exhaustion doctrine: The Supreme Court has held that if agency action is final under §704, no further exhaustion is required and review is available immediately. Under §704, exhaustion is required only of those remedies expressly required by statute or agency rule.

E. Mootness

A case is moot if there is no longer a live controversy between the parties. For example, if a party is no longer subject to an agency rule or if the agency repeals the rule, a claim for judicial review of the rule may be moot. There are exceptions to mootness: a claim may be heard despite mootness if the claim is "capable of repetition yet evading review" or when the defendant voluntarily ceases the challenged conduct but remains free to resume it.

CHAPTER 4

JUDICIAL REVIEW OF ADMINISTRATIVE DECISIONS

I. STANDARDS OF JUDICIAL REVIEW UNDER THE APA

APA standards of judicial review govern unless the agency's enabling act contains a provision establishing a standard of review that differs from the applicable APA standard.

A. APA §706 and Standards of Review

APA §706(2)(D) applies the substantial evidence test to formal adjudication and formal rulemaking.

APA §706(2)(E) applies de novo review when (1) "the [agency] action is adjudicatory in nature and the agency factfinding procedures are inadequate" or (2) "issues that were not before the agency are raised in a proceeding to enforce nonadjudicatory agency action."

APA §706 (2)(A) provides that any agency action should be set aside if it is "arbitrary, capricious, an abuse of discretion, or otherwise not in accordance with law." The arbitrary and capricious test contains no limitation on its applicability, and thus it applies to all reviewable administrative actions. Because it is the most deferential standard of review, parties challenging administrative action prefer de novo or substantial evidence review.

B. The Record on Review

APA §706 requires reviewing courts to examine the "whole record." The record consists of the material the agency had before it when it made its decision — not support created after the agency made its decision. The reviewing court looks at the whole record, not just the evidence supporting the agency's decision.

II. THE SUBSTANTIAL EVIDENCE TEST

The substantial evidence test, which governs review of formal agency adjudication and formal rulemaking, is the same standard that governs whether a judge should submit an issue to a jury rather than direct a verdict. That standard is whether such relevant evidence exists as a reasonable mind might accept as adequate to support a conclusion. The "whole record" requirement means that a decision might fail the substantial evidence test even though it is supported by some evidence, when that evidence is overwhelmed by evidence to the contrary.

A. Witness Credibility

When an agency's decision is based, in whole or in part, on the credibility of the witnesses, the agency's decision is entitled to great deference because the reviewing court reviews only the paper record, without the opportunity to observe the demeanor of the witnesses.

B. Agency Reversals of ALJ Decisions

When an agency reverses the decision of the trier of fact on appeal within the agency, the initial decision is part of the "whole record," and the reviewing court must take the reversal into account in deciding whether the agency's decision is supported by substantial evidence.

III. DE NOVO REVIEW OF QUESTIONS OF FACT

Where agency adjudicatory factfinding procedures are inadequate or when new factual issues arise in an action to enforce nonadjudicatory agency action, the regulated party might be entitled to de novo review of the facts. De novo review means that the facts are retried in the court, and no deference is paid to agency factual conclusions.

IV. REVIEW OF QUESTIONS OF LAW

There are competing traditions regarding judicial review of agency conclusions of law — one under which courts review questions of law de novo and another under which courts defer to agency interpretations of the statutes they administer. Courts have traditionally shown the greatest deference to agency decisions involving the applications of law to particular facts. Although the Court no longer distinguishes between issues of statutory authority to regulate and other statutory issues, traditionally courts have decided issues of agency statutory authority without deferring to the agency's interpretation of its enabling act.

A. *Chevron*

In *Chevron, U.S.A., Inc. v. Natural Resources Defense Council, Inc.,* 467 U.S. 837 (1984), the Court stated that unless Congress has directly spoken to the precise issue in question, courts should defer to agencies on pure questions of statutory interpretation as long as the agency arrived at a reasonable or permissible construction of the statute.

B. **Less Deferential** *Chevron:* **Cardoza-Fonseca**

The Court sometimes states that under *Chevron,* the reviewing court should attempt to ascertain Congress's intent using "traditional tools of statutory construction." These include the language, structure, purpose, and legislative history of the statute being construed, and other interpretive devices such as the canons of statutory interpretation. *See INS v. Cardoza-Fonseca,* 480 U.S. 421, 447 (1987).

C. *Chevron:* **Permissible Construction**

An agency's interpretation is permissible under *Chevron* if it is "a sufficiently rational one to preclude a court from substituting its judgment for that of the [agency]." *Young v. Community Nutrition Institute,* 476 U.S. 974, 981 (1986). This is very deferential.

D. **When** *Chevron* **Applies**

Chevron applies to agency statutory interpretations rendered in relatively formal settings such as rulemaking and adjudication. Under *United States v. Mead Corp.,* 533 U.S. 218 (2001), it does not apply to agency statutory interpretations rendered less formally, such as in a ruling letter. In such cases, *Skidmore* deference may apply. Under *Skidmore*, courts defer to agency statutory interpretations on a sliding scale based on the formality of the process, the importance of agency expertise, and the degree to which the agency's reasoning is persuasive.

V. REVIEW OF QUESTIONS OF POLICY

1. **Informal rulemaking and informal agency action:** Courts review most agency policy decisions under the arbitrary and capricious test, which applies to informal rulemaking and informal agency action. The arbitrary and capricious test requires that agencies make decisions:

    1. "based on a consideration of the relevant factors," including alternatives to the agency's proposal;

    2. without "a clear error of judgment"; and

    3. under the correct legal standard.

The Court has also stated that:

> **4.** while the arbitrary and capricious inquiry is "searching and careful,"
>
> **5.** the standard of review is "a narrow one. The court is not empowered to substitute its judgment for that of the agency."

Citizens to Preserve Overton Park v. Volpe, 401 U.S. 402, 416-17 (1971).

As proof that they considered all relevant factors, courts require agencies to explain their decisions on major issues raised during the decisionmaking process.

2. **The special case of the standard of review of deregulation:** Deregulation is normally reviewed under the same test that applies to the initial promulgation of the regulation being relaxed or rescinded. In most cases of informal rulemaking, this means the arbitrary and capricious test. The Court has rejected arguments that deregulation decisions should be reviewed under the same standard that governs a refusal to regulate in the first place.

VI. REMEDIES ON JUDICIAL REVIEW

Reviewing courts have the power under APA §706 to "hold unlawful and set aside" agency action found not to meet the applicable standard of review. However, courts often remand matters to the agency for further consideration without ordering the agency to change its decision. This gives agencies the opportunity to cure any defects identified on judicial review.

CHAPTER 5

AGENCY CHOICE OF POLICYMAKING MODE

I. CONSTITUTIONAL CONSTRAINTS ON CHOICE OF POLICYMAKING MODE

In most cases the choice between rulemaking and adjudication is left to Congress or to the agency under delegation from Congress. When an agency makes a decision applicable generally to an entire class of parties, a legislative procedure is sufficient to satisfy due process. *See Bi-Metallic Investment Co. v. State Board of Equalization*, 239 U.S. 441 (1915). However, under *Londoner v. Denver*, 210 U.S. 373 (1908), due process requires an adjudicatory hearing when the agency's decision is particularized to the situation of a regulated party.

II. CHOICE OF POLICYMAKING PROCEDURE

The APA divides all agency action into two models—rulemaking and adjudication—but says very little about when each is required. Agencies must employ an adjudicatory process to issue orders against regulated parties. Agencies make rule-like determinations in both rulemaking and adjudication, and either is proper as long as the agency has the power to use the particular procedure and all procedural requirements are observed.

A. Agency Discretion to Make Policy by Rule

Rulemaking is the preferred policymaking method for agencies because it allows agencies to make clear, comprehensive decisions in a legislative process in which the agency can benefit from extensive public input and thus make better policy decisions. Rulemaking is also fair because it establishes rules that govern all regulated parties at once rather than singling out parties at different times, which may occur when an agency brings an enforcement action against one regulated party at a time.

B. Rulemaking and the Right to a Hearing

Agencies often use rulemaking to determine whether particular conduct violates a regulatory statute. Regulated parties have argued that when Congress establishes a hearing process to determine regulatory violations, the rulemaking violates their right to a hearing on all issues. This argument is usually rejected with a caveat that the agency must provide an opportunity for the party to argue that the rule should not apply in the particular case.

C. Agency Power to Make Policy by Adjudication

Agencies often announce new rules of decision in an opinion arising from an adjudication. This practice has been challenged on the ground that the APA's definitions require rulemaking as the procedure for formulating general rules. The Supreme Court has rejected these challenges, although not definitively, stating that the choice between adjudication and rulemaking lies largely within the discretion of the agency.

III. INFORMAL POLICYMAKING

A. Exemptions From §553

APA §553 exempts from all of its requirements rules that are in the areas of the military, foreign affairs, agency management, personnel, public property, loans, grants, benefits, and contracts. Section 553 also exempts, from its notice and comment requirements, nonlegislative rules such as interpretative rules, general statements of policy, and rules of agency organization or practice. Further, §553(b) allows agencies to dispense with notice and comment procedures when it finds that such procedures are "impracticable, unnecessary or contrary to the public interest."

1. **Nonlegislative rule:** A nonlegislative rule is a rule that has no legal effect. Rather, it interprets existing legal obligations (interpretative rule) or states the agency's view on a matter of policy without creating legal rights or obligations (general statement of policy). Nonlegislative rules must be published in the Federal Register. Agencies may not give legal effect to nonlegislative rules.

B. Policymaking by Manual or Other Internal Document

When an agency makes policy without going through either rulemaking or adjudication, the APA requires that any rule be published in the Federal Register or it may not be used against any party not having actual notice of it. APA §552(a)(1). *See Morton v. Ruiz*, 415 U.S. 199 (1974).

C. Agencies' Obligation to Follow Their Own Procedural Rules

Agencies must follow any procedural rules they have formally adopted through notice and comment procedures, but informally adopted rules may be ignored unless a party that the agency intended to benefit detrimentally relied upon the informally adopted procedural rule. *See American Freight Lines v. Black Ball Freight Service*, 397 U.S. 532 (1970); *Schweiker v. Hansen*, 450 U.S. 785 (1981).

D. Informal Policymaking Generally: When May an Agency Act Without Adjudication or Rulemaking?

While agencies often decide policy matters and grant or deny applications or petitions informally (without using either an adjudicatory or rulemaking procedure), the statutory basis for this widespread practice is unclear. Because the APA appears to divide all agency actions between rulemaking and adjudication, this informal decisionmaking is often referred to as "informal adjudication." When an agency makes a decision informally, the only procedural requirements are notice of the decision and a brief statement of the reasons for the decision. *See* APA §555(e).

CHAPTER 6

APA RULEMAKING PROCEDURES

I. APA §553 INFORMAL ("NOTICE AND COMMENT") RULEMAKING PROCEDURES

A. Basic Requirements of Informal Rulemaking

The basic requirements of informal rulemaking are: published notice of the proposed rulemaking, opportunity for public comment and, after consideration of the comments, publication of the final rule together with a concise general statement of the rule's basis and purpose.

B. Notice

APA §553 requires notice of either the text of a proposed regulation or a description of the subjects or issues involved in the rulemaking. To prevent agencies from proposing one rule and then promulgating a completely different one, courts have required that the rules ultimately adopted be the logical outgrowth of the proposal, that they not substantially depart from the original proposal, or that the final rule may not materially alter the proposal. The cure for inadequate notice is a new notice and a new comment period.

C. Meaningful Opportunity to Submit Comments

Some courts have interpreted APA §553(c)'s requirement that interested parties be allowed to submit comments on proposed rules to require a "meaningful" opportunity to participate. These courts have required agencies to provide notice of any data or studies upon which the agency relies. *See United States v. Nova Scotia Food Prods. Corp.,* 568 F.2d 240 (2d Cir. 1977); *National Black Media Coalition v. FCC,* 791 F.2d 1016 (2d Cir. 1986). Although nothing in the APA explicitly requires it, courts have held that for the opportunity to participate to be meaningful, interested persons must be allowed to respond to opposing comments.

D. The Problem of Ex Parte Contacts in Rulemaking

Ex parte contacts consist of communications from interested parties to administrators outside the formalities of the comment process. While such contacts are barred in formal adjudication and formal rulemaking, the APA does not bar ex parte contacts in informal rulemaking.

1. **Ban on ex parte contacts:** While some courts hold that ex parte contacts are generally not barred in informal rulemaking, some courts have ruled that ex parte contacts should not be allowed because they threaten the ability of other interested parties to participate meaningfully in the rulemaking process. Some courts suggest that agencies should consider only the comments presented through the notice and comment process because ex parte comments threaten the court's ability, on judicial review, to examine the true basis of agency decisions. Other courts have confined the ban on ex parte contacts to rulemakings that involve competing claims to a valuable privilege.

2. **Remedy for ex parte contacts:** Even courts holding that ex parte contacts should not occur recognize that the realities of the political process mean that such contacts may occur. Thus, courts have held that if ex parte contacts do occur, any documents received and a summary of oral communications should be placed on the record.

3. **Intragovernmental ex parte contacts:** The President, as chief executive, has a right to receive information from administrative officials regarding pending rulemakings, and he also has a right to give input on the substance of rulemakings. It may also be appropriate for members of Congress to represent the interests of their constituents through ex parte contacts as long as they do not raise extraneous matters to pressure the agency in the rulemaking process.

E. Prejudgment in Rulemaking

A decisionmaker in a rulemaking may be disqualified if it is shown by clear and convincing evidence that the decisionmaker has prejudged the issues to such a great extent that he or she has an unalterably closed mind, and thus will not consider the comments submitted in the rulemaking process. *See Association of National Advertisers, Inc. v. FTC,* 627 F.2d 1151 (D.C. Cir. 1979), *cert. denied,* 447 U.S. 921 (1980).

F. The Concise General Statement

APA §553 requires agencies to explain their rules with a "concise general statement of their basis and purpose." The statement must respond to substantial issues raised by the comments and state the agency's views on major issues of law and policy.

G. Publication of Final Rules

Agencies must publish final rules in the Federal Register. If a rule is not properly published, the rule is ineffective as to any party without actual notice of the rule. APA §552.

H. Hybrid Rulemaking

Some enabling acts impose procedural requirements in addition to those included in §553. They usually consist of discovery, cross-examination of experts, and additional comment periods so that interested parties could comment on adverse comments submitted. Courts also imposed such requirements in complex rulemakings when they viewed §553 procedures as inadequate. In *Vermont Yankee Nuclear Power Corp. v. NRDC,* 435 U.S. 519 (1978), the Supreme Court ruled that courts may not require procedures in addition to those specified in either the APA or an enabling act because uncertainty over the correct level of procedure would lead agencies to overproceduralize, losing the benefits of the streamlined rulemaking process. This calls into question judicial imposition of the ban on ex parte communications in rulemakings as well as other judicially imposed procedural requirements.

II. FORMAL RULEMAKING PROCEDURES: THE ADDITIONAL REQUIREMENTS OF APA §§556 AND 557

A. When Is Formal Rulemaking Required?

Formal rulemaking, which is rulemaking conducted in a formal, adjudicatory procedure, is required when the agency's enabling act requires rules to be made "on the record after opportunity for an agency hearing." Because formal rulemaking is a cumbersome procedure, courts are loath to find that it is required and agencies rarely use it.

B. Formal Rulemaking Procedures

Formal rulemaking is conducted like a trial, with an administrative law judge or agency head presiding. Ex parte communications are prohibited. Parties are entitled to present their cases by oral or documentary evidence, and they are entitled to cross-examine opposing witnesses. The record produced at the hearing is the exclusive record for decision in formal rulemaking, and a detailed decision with findings of fact and conclusions of law is required.

III. NEGOTIATED RULEMAKING

Under the Negotiated Rulemaking Act, agencies may formulate proposed rules through a process of formal negotiations among interested parties. If negotiations are successful, the agency normally proposes a rule in line with the negotiated consensus. Such rules are subject to normal notice and comment procedures, and the agency is free to change its mind and promulgate a final rule that differs from the rule agreed to in negotiations.

IV. DIRECT FINAL RULEMAKING

If no adverse comments are expected, some agencies have employed a procedure called "direct final rulemaking" under which an agency publishes a final rule and specifies that it will go into effect unless the agency receives adverse comments. If the agency receives adverse comments, the direct final rulemaking is canceled, and the agency conducts a normal notice and comment process. While direct final rulemaking has not been tested in court, it will probably be upheld as a method for promulgating legislative rules as long as the receipt of adverse comments triggers notice and comment procedures.

CHAPTER 7

AGENCY ADJUDICATION AND DUE PROCESS

I. ARTICLE III CONSTITUTIONAL LIMITS ON AGENCY ADJUDICATION

Agency adjudication appears to violate Article III's vesting of the judicial power of the United States in the federal courts. However, the federal courts have approved agency adjudication when it occurs under circumstances thought not to threaten the policies and values underlying Article III.

Agency adjudication is most clearly permissible in public rights disputes, which are disputes between a private party and the government over such things as licenses or benefits. More recently, the Supreme Court has approved of agency adjudication of disputes between two private parties where the rights involved arise out of or are closely associated with a federal regulatory scheme and where the essential attributes of judicial power remain in the federal courts so that the role of the federal courts in the government is not threatened. The Court has found it important that agency orders must be enforced in court, and the parties have a choice between an Article III court and a non-Article III tribunal. The Court has rejected Justice Brennan's view that non-Article III adjudication is permissible only in the three narrow categories of territorial courts, military courts, and public rights disputes. *See Community Futures Trading Comm'n v. Schor,* 478 U.S. 833, 859 (1986) (Brennan, J. dissenting).

II. DUE PROCESS AND THE ADJUDICATORY HEARING

A. Property Interests

The first question in any due process dispute is whether the claim involves a protected interest, i.e., life, liberty, or property. While at one time interests such as government benefits were thought of as gratuities that could be withdrawn at any time, today such interests are considered property interests if claims to the benefit are evaluated under a definite set of criteria that create an entitlement to the benefit. In the absence of an explicit entitlement, less formal assurances or state practices may create an entitlement.

B. "Bitter With the Sweet"

In *Arnett v. Kennedy,* 416 U.S. 134 (1974), Justice Rehnquist, joined by two other members of the Court, argued that a civil service employee with a for-cause termination provision (the "sweet") should receive only the minimal process (the "bitter") specified in the statute granting the for-cause entitlement. A majority of the Court rejected this argument, adhering to *Roth*'s separation of procedure from substance."

C. Liberty

Some liberty interests are created, like property interests, by external law that creates an entitlement. For example, while prisoners have no constitutional right to parole, if state law creates an entitlement to parole, then a liberty interest is created and due process standards govern the procedures employed at parole hearings. Other liberty interests, such as the right to freedom of movement, are recognized as part of the constitutional definition of liberty and are thus created by the Due Process Clause itself.

D. Determining What Process Is Due

How much process is due is determined by applying the *Mathews v. Eldridge* balancing test and asking whether the procedures already provided are adequate. The *Mathews v. Eldridge* balancing test considers (1) the strength of the private interest affected by the government action; (2) the risk of an erroneous deprivation if additional procedure is not afforded; and (3) the government's interest in proceeding with no more process than already afforded.

Sometimes, alternatives to a trial-like hearing in the agency in advance of the adverse action are held to satisfy due process. These alternatives include common law remedies, postdeprivation remedies more generally, and a consultative model of procedure. Agencies may not impose legally binding orders on regulated parties without following due process.

E. The Right to a Neutral Decisionmaker

1. **Bias:** Due process is violated if a decisionmaker has a pecuniary interest in the outcome of the adjudication. Pecuniary interests can be direct, such as a decisionmaker who receives a portion of any fines levied in an adjudication, or indirect, such as a decisionmaker in competition with those subject to the agency enforcement. Bias may also exist if a decisionmaker feels pressure from agency superiors to decide in a particular way.

2. **Prejudgment:** Due process is violated if it appears that a decisionmaker in an adjudication has, in some measure, prejudged the facts or law of a particular case prior to hearing it.

III. STATUTORY HEARING RIGHTS

Many statutes grant the right to a hearing to determine matters such as licenses and government benefits.

A. The Statutorily Required Hearing Must Be Genuine

When a statute grants an applicant a hearing on an application for a government benefit or license, the hearing must provide the applicant with a genuine opportunity to prevail. Under *Ashbacker*, the agency may not make it nearly impossible for the applicant to prevail before holding the hearing. *See Ashbacker Radio Corp. v. FCC,* 326 U.S. 327 (1945).

B. Substantive Standards That Limit Hearings

Agencies with the power to engage in rulemaking may adopt substantive rules that limit the issues addressed at a statutorily prescribed hearing. The rules must be substantively valid. Because these rules are in tension with the party's statutory right to a hearing, courts have required that agencies provide an opportunity for parties to argue that a rule does not, or should not, apply to the particular case.

C. Applications That Establish Ineligibility

In *United States v. Storer Broadcasting Co.,* 351 U.S. 192 (1956), the Court held that the Federal Communications Commission (FCC) is free to deny an application without a hearing when the application itself reveals that the license would be denied under a substantively valid statute or regulation.

D. The Irrebuttable Presumption Doctrine

The irrebuttable presumption doctrine held that when there was a liberty or property interest at stake, due process required a hearing on all issues, and a statute could not preclude a hearing on a central issue. This doctrine proved unworkable, and it was abandoned in *Weinberger v. Salfi,* 422 U.S. 749 (1975), when the Court upheld a provision of the Social Security Act that excluded widows who were married to a deceased worker for shorter than nine months from eligibility for survivors' benefits against a challenge that the statute created an irrebuttable presumption that a marriage shorter than nine months was a sham.

CHAPTER 8

SUBSTANTIVE POLICYMAKING IN AGENCIES

I. PERMISSIBLE CONSIDERATIONS IN AGENCY POLICYMAKING

Agencies are required to consider only the factors made relevant by their enabling acts and by other generally applicable statutes such as the National Environmental Policy Act (NEPA). Agencies should make policy by applying their expertise, in a reasoned fashion, to the factors made statutorily relevant. Agencies should not take factors into account that are not within the considerations made relevant by statute or valid regulation.

II. COST-BENEFIT ANALYSIS

Cost-benefit analysis promotes reasoned decisionmaking by forcing agencies to quantify the effects of their actions in a more concrete fashion. While it has been argued that agencies should be required to conduct cost-benefit analysis regarding their major policy decisions and should not adopt a policy unless the benefits outweigh the costs, courts will not require cost-benefit analysis unless statutorily required. Courts have not read general standards such as "reasonably necessary or appropriate" as requiring cost-benefit analysis, perhaps in part because many costs and benefits are difficult to quantify and because Congress appears to prefer values other than efficiency in many regulatory programs.

III. IMPACT STATEMENTS

Another method of forcing agencies to focus on the effects of their actions is to require the agency to prepare an impact statement, such as an environmental impact statement or a small business regulatory impact statement. Impact statements improve decision-making and provide an opportunity for opponents of the agency's plan to put pressure on the agency to change or abandon its plans due to undesirable effects.

A. Environmental Impact Statements Under NEPA

NEPA requires federal agencies to prepare Environmental Impact Statements (EIS) regarding "major Federal actions significantly affecting the quality of the human environment." The EIS must detail the effects and include consideration of alternatives.

B. Environmental Effects

In addition to traditional environmental effects, NEPA covers a broad range of effects on the human environment, such as displacement of social institutions and concentration of low-income residents in a neighborhood. For NEPA to apply, there must be a physical alteration of the environment and the matter must be within the agency's control.

C. NEPA Is Essentially Procedural

The EIS must be part of the record during agency consideration of its action, and courts have held that the agency must consider the environmental effects. Nothing in NEPA, however, requires that agency action be changed or abandoned due to environmental effects.

IV. CONSISTENCY AND CLARITY REQUIREMENTS

Courts have, on judicial review, required agencies to operate under clearly stated substantive criteria and have required agencies to treat like cases alike.

A. Clarity

The clarity cases, which are in tension with decisions allowing agencies the discretion to decide issues on a case-by-case basis, hold that agency action may be taken only pursuant to clear criteria. Some courts have held that where property or liberty interests are at stake, clarity is required by due process.

B. Agency Decisions Are Judged on the Reasons Stated by the Agency

Related to the clarity requirement is the well-established doctrine that agency decisions are evaluated, on judicial review, based on the reasons given by the agency at the time the decision was made, not on reasons first offered on judicial review.

C. Consistency

Agencies are required to be consistent, i.e., to treat like cases alike, and must offer an explanation, when they treat like cases differently.

D. Agencies Must Follow Their Own Rules

Agencies are required to follow their own rules, whether those rules have been adopted in a rulemaking proceeding or announced in the course of an agency adjudication, unless the agency has validly changed its rule. Agencies must apply their rules as written and may not change their rules by applying a rule in a manner inconsistent with the rule as written. *See Allentown Mack Sales and Service, Inc. v. NLRB*, 522 U.S. 359 (1998). However, courts often allow agencies to ignore rules that have not been formally adopted in a rulemaking or adjudication.

E. Estoppel and Administrative Agencies

Except in extreme circumstances and where government funds are not involved, agencies are not estopped by the conduct or statements of agency officials. For example, if an agency official gives erroneous advice by misstating the eligibility requirements for a government program, the erroneous advice does not estop the agency from relying upon the program's actual requirements to deny claims.

F. Nonacquiescence

Agencies sometimes refuse to acquiesce to legal rulings by lower federal courts. In such cases, the agency may follow the ruling in the circuit in which it was rendered but will adhere to its position in other courts with the possibility of prevailing with a favorable ruling in the Supreme Court. While intercircuit nonacquiescence seems appropriate in some circumstances, intracircuit nonacquiescence, in which an agency refuses to follow a decision of the court of appeals even within the circuit that rendered the decision, is difficult to defend.

CHAPTER 9

AGENCY ENFORCEMENT AND LICENSING

I. PROSECUTORIAL DISCRETION

A. Decisions Not to Prosecute or Regulate

Unless an enabling act contains standards under which an agency is required to prosecute a violator or regulate in an area, a decision not to prosecute or regulate is not reviewable. By and large, courts have concluded that the agency should be left to decide, in its expert judgment, which enforcement actions present the best use of agency resources.

B. Potential Problems with Agency Prosecutorial Discretion

Unreviewable agency prosecutorial discretion presents the potential for subversion of congressional intent by applying different priorities than those that led Congress to pass the agency's enabling act. Agency prosecutorial discretion may allow an agency to play political favorites and may also lead the agency to select only easy targets for prosecution, leaving serious violations unaddressed.

C. Discriminatory Enforcement

Subjects of agency enforcement sometimes claim that although they may have violated regulatory norms, the agency should not issue an enforcement order against them unless and until the agency issues enforcement orders against others (for example, competitors) engaged in the same practice. The standard for deciding whether a court should preclude an agency from enforcing an order until the agency orders others in the industry to halt the same practice is "patent abuse of discretion" — a very difficult standard to meet. As long as an agency can articulate a rational basis for its actions, the order will be enforced.

D. Discriminatory Imposition of Sanctions

Courts have rejected claims that agencies have imposed overly harsh sanctions for violations, either when compared to sanctions imposed on others, or under agency policy regarding sanctions. The Supreme Court has held that absent statutory restrictions, an agency is free to impose whatever sanctions are within its statutory power.

E. Constitutionally Based Claims of Discriminatory Enforcement

An agency violates equal protection if it selects its enforcement targets based on a suspect classification. *See Yick Wo v. Hopkins,* 118 U.S. 356 (1886). When outspoken criticism of an agency or the program the agency administers triggers enforcement, regulated parties have unsuccessfully argued that the prosecution punishes or chills speech in violation of the First Amendment.

II. LICENSING AND RATEMAKING

A. Occupational Licensing

Doctors, lawyers, optometrists, pharmacists, hair stylists, truck drivers, and many other professionals must obtain licenses from the state in order to practice their professions.

1. Licenses are property protected by due process: Because discernible standards normally govern the grant, denial, renewal, and revocation of professional licenses, such licenses are protected by due process as property.

2. Bias due to self-interest: The problem of self-regulation: Occupational licensing often presents the potential for bias due to self-interest because the licensing board may be dominated by one segment of a profession that seeks to avoid competition from another segment. If the members of the board have an interest in the outcome of a proceeding before it, due process may preclude them from hearing it.

B. Broadcast Licensing Procedures

1. "Public interest" standard for granting licenses: The FCC decides whether to grant a broadcast license based on the very discretionary standard of "public interest, convenience, and necessity."

2. Broadcast licensing hearing requirements: The FCC is required to hold a full adjudicatory hearing before rejecting an application for a broadcast license.

3. **Mutually exclusive applications: The *Ashbacker* rule:** When two applicants file competing applications, the FCC may not grant one of the applications without holding a hearing on the other. *See Ashbacker Radio Corp. v. FCC*, 326 U.S. 327 (1945). To meet this obligation, the FCC holds comparative hearings in which the relative merits of applicants are judged on a variety of factors such as diversification of ownership, involvement of ownership in the management of the station, the quality of proposed programming, and the character of the applicants. While comparative hearings were formerly held on renewal applications, recent legislation has created an entitlement to renewal absent inferior service or other violations by the incumbent licensee.

4. **Restricting the scope of hearings by rule: *Storer:*** In *United States v. Storer Broadcasting Co.,* 351 U.S. 192 (1956), the Court held that the FCC may make the "public interest, convenience, and necessity" standard more specific with rules, such as multiple ownership rules that restrict the number of stations owned by a licensee. The Court held that it did not violate the right to a full hearing to deny a license based on noncompliance with an FCC rule.

C. Ratemaking Principles and Procedures

Ratemaking is the procedure for setting rates in regulated industries such as electric power and telephone. Ratemaking has been conducted according to three different models: one in which rates set by the company are subject to challenge as "unreasonable," one in which rates are prescribed in a comprehensive formal ratemaking process, and one in which the company files tariffs that are barely examined by the agency unless someone challenges them.

CHAPTER **10**

AGENCY INFORMATION GATHERING

I. INSPECTIONS

Many agencies monitor compliance with regulatory requirements by inspecting the subjects of regulation. To do so, the agency must have authority to inspect. Further, agencies are subject to constitutional constraints on information gathering.

A. Administrative Authority to Inspect Regulated Businesses

The APA prohibits agencies from conducting inspections, or otherwise gathering information, without legal authority. APA §555(c).

B. Constitutional Constraints on Agency Inspection

Agency inspections are subject to constitutional constraints, most notably those imposed by the Fourth Amendment. However, probable cause (in the criminal law sense) is not required for warrants to conduct inspections. In "pervasively regulated businesses," warrants may be unnecessary.

1. **Normally, a warrant is required:** Under normal circumstances, a warrant is required before government agents may enter and inspect a business to monitor compliance with regulatory requirements.

2. **Warrants for administrative inspections may issue without probable cause:** An agency may obtain a warrant merely by showing that normal legislative or administrative standards for conducting an inspection are met. The agency does not need probable cause.

3. **Pervasively regulated businesses:** In cases where substantial regulatory interest would be threatened by imposing a warrant requirement, no warrant is required to inspect the premises of a business that is subject to pervasive regulation.

C. Regulatory Inspections of Homes

Recipients of government benefits may be required to allow welfare caseworkers to inspect their homes as a condition of continued benefits. Also, warrants to inspect a home for compliance with a building code do not require probable cause in the criminal sense. Rather, warrants may issue if the agency establishes that the inspection is part of its normal regulatory scheme to monitor compliance with the relevant code. Finally, probation officers may, without a warrant or probable cause, search the homes of convicted criminals who have been placed on probation.

D. Drug Testing

Drug testing programs are evaluated according to several factors, including the expectation of privacy of the individual tested, the degree to which the testing program invades that privacy, the importance of the governmental interest underlying the testing program, and the degree to which the testing program's standards ameliorate the potential for arbitrary selection of individuals to be tested.

II. PRODUCTION OF INFORMATION AND DOCUMENTS

A. Agency Requests for Information or Documents

An agency may require regulated parties to provide information or documents as long as the demand is not too indefinite or burdensome, and the information sought is reasonably relevant to a matter of legitimate agency concern. Subjects of investigations normally cannot test the agency's jurisdiction in a proceeding to enforce a subpoena.

B. Disclosure of Privileged Information or Trade Secrets

It is unclear whether agencies must respect recognized privileges such as the attorney-client privilege, the doctor-patient privilege, and the husband-wife privilege. Corporations, other entities (such as labor unions and partnerships), and the custodians of records for such entities, have no Fifth Amendment privilege against providing the government with information or documents. The government may be required, under the Takings Clause, to compensate a regulated party whose trade secret information is disclosed.

III. THE PAPERWORK REDUCTION ACT

Before an agency may promulgate a new request for information, the agency must submit a proposal to Office of Information and Regulatory Affairs (OIRA) within the Office of Management and Budget (OMB). OIRA may reject the agency's proposal if it finds that the agency does not have a legitimate need for the information. The Paperwork Reduction Act (PRA) does not apply to requirements that one regulated party disclose information directly to another party.

CHAPTER 11

PRIVATE ENFORCEMENT OF REGULATORY NORMS AND PREEMPTION

I. THE CITIZENS' SUIT

A. Suits Against Violators

Citizens' suit provisions typically authorize "any citizen" or "any person" to seek damages, an injunction, or both against violations of the relevant statute by private parties and by government. This citizens' suit provision does not authorize a suit against the government for regulatory errors but only for conduct that violates the substance of a regulatory program, such as pollution by the government in violation of an environmental statute.

B. Suits Against the Government as Regulator

Citizens' suit provisions typically provide for actions in the nature of mandamus against regulators when it is alleged that they have not fulfilled nondiscretionary regulatory duties. This provision is not a substitute for judicial review and may not be used to examine the substance of agency action.

C. Standing Problems in Citizens' Suits

Plaintiffs in citizens' suits must meet all Article III standing requirements. Citizens' suit provisions may, however, overrule prudential limits on standing and place all "citizens" within the zone of interests of the relevant regulatory program.

II. IMPLIED PRIVATE RIGHTS OF ACTION

If congressional intent to do so exists, a federal court may imply a right of action so that a private party can sue another private party for violating a regulatory statute even if the regulatory statute itself provides only for enforcement by a federal agency. Contrary to older cases, the recent cases allow rights of action to be implied only if it appears that Congress intended courts to do so. The focus on congressional intent arises from arguments that those courts that implied rights of action without evidence of such intent were usurping Congress's legislative function.

III. ALTERNATIVE STATE REMEDIES AND REGULATORY PREEMPTION

A. Preemption of State Remedies

There is a presumption, rooted in federalism concerns, that state law is not preempted unless Congress's intent to do so is clear. Nonetheless, Congress may preempt state law explicitly, by providing in a statute that state law is preempted, or implicitly, by creating federal law that is so comprehensive it appears that Congress must have intended to displace state law that is within the "field" occupied by Congress. Further, state law in actual conflict with federal law, or which stands as an obstacle to the realization of federal policy, is preempted.

B. The Primary Jurisdiction Doctrine

The primary jurisdiction doctrine requires that a claim within the substantive jurisdiction of an agency must be heard first by that agency even if the facts give rise to a claim otherwise cognizable in a court. A savings clause in a regulatory statute may prevent the primary jurisdiction doctrine from operating.

CHAPTER 12

LIABILITY OF AGENCIES AND OFFICIALS

I. SOVEREIGN IMMUNITY AND SUITS AGAINST FEDERAL AGENTS AND AGENCIES

A. Common-law Sovereign Immunity

At common law, sovereign immunity barred damages actions against the government and government officials acting in their official capacities unless the government consented to the suit.

B. The Federal Tort Claims Act

The Federal Tort Claims Act (FTCA) waived the sovereign immunity of the federal government for negligent or otherwise wrongful acts or omissions by the United States government or its employees. The FTCA creates federal government liability for "tort claims . . . in the same manner and to the same extent as a private individual under like circumstances." 28 U.S.C. §2674. The FTCA is often used to pursue an action for damages when the conduct of administrators is allegedly tortious.

C. Exceptions to FTCA Liability

The FTCA contains numerous exceptions and limitations, the most important of which is the discretionary-function exception. The Supreme Court has defined the discretionary-function exception as exempting actions from liability when the official has choice and when the action involves the "permissible exercise of policy judgment." In addition to law and policymaking functions, the courts have held that the discretionary-functions exception bars liability for errors in the planning stages of government operations. The Court has also been very skeptical of claims that the government should be held liable for negligence in performing inspections and similar regulatory functions.

D. The *Feres* Doctrine

The Supreme Court has created a nonstatutory exception to the FTCA, called the "*Feres* Doctrine," for military activities. This doctrine basically bars all claims that are "incident to service" in the armed forces.

II. LIABILITY OF INDIVIDUAL FEDERAL OFFICIALS

A. Common-law Immunities of Government Officials

In many situations, government officials are privileged to engage in conduct that, if performed by a private party, would be tortious. The courts have also recognized immunity from tort liability for federal government officials acting within the scope of their duties. Further, if a claim against a federal government official falls within the scope of the FTCA, the government is substituted as defendant, and the individual official is released from liability.

B. Judicially Created Constitutional Tort Liability

The Supreme Court, in *Bivens v. Six Unknown Named Agents of Federal Bureau of Narcotics,* 403 U.S. 388 (1971), created a damages action against federal officials for constitutional torts.

1. **Exceptions to *Bivens:*** The *Bivens* action is not available when there are "special factors counseling hesitation in the absence of affirmative action by Congress," or when Congress has provided an alternative remedy that it explicitly declared to be a *substitute* for the *Bivens* action. The existence of a comprehensive alternative remedial scheme has been considered a special factor counseling hesitation.

2. **Immunities in *Bivens* actions:** Administrative officials performing judicial, legislative, and prosecutorial functions are absolutely immune from damages because at common law, judges, legislators, and prosecutors were absolutely immune from damages. Officials performing functions not traditionally accorded an absolute immunity are protected by a qualified immunity. A plaintiff can overcome the qualified immunity by showing that the defendant violated a clearly established constitutional right of which a reasonable official should have known.

III. LIABILITY OF STATE AND LOCAL GOVERNMENT OFFICIALS

State and local government officials can be sued in federal court under 42 U.S.C. §1983 for damages and injunctive relief for conduct violating the federal Constitution and laws.

A. Eleventh Amendment

The Eleventh Amendment, as interpreted and applied by the Supreme Court, prohibits the federal courts from awarding damages against states and state government agencies. State officials can be enjoined from violating federal law and state officials can be held personally liable for damages, to be paid out of their own pockets.

B. "And Laws" Actions

Section 1983 provides a cause of action against state officials who violate federal statutory law. However, when the federal statute contains a comprehensive remedial scheme that includes its own private right of action against violations, the Supreme Court has held that plaintiffs must use the particular statutory remedy and not the more general §1983 action. The Court has also held that the §1983 remedy for violating a federal statute is not available when the federal statute creates no enforceable rights.

C. Immunities

Defendants in §1983 actions are protected by the same immunities that the courts have applied in *Bivens* actions.

D. Municipal Liability

Municipalities are "persons" subject to suit under §1983, but they may be held liable only for municipal policy or custom and may not be held liable on a vicarious liability theory for the constitutional violations of their employees.

CHAPTER 13

FREEDOM OF INFORMATION AND OPEN MEETINGS

I. THE FREEDOM OF INFORMATION ACT (FOIA)

A. Public Right of Access to Agency Records

FOIA requires that agencies publish certain matters and allow public inspection, upon request, of all other "records" unless the records sought fall within one of FOIA's exceptions.

1. **Agency records:** Agency records are those records that are created or obtained by the agency in the course of doing the agency's work and in the control of the agency at the time of the FOIA request.

2. **Records "wrongfully withheld":** FOIA creates a legal claim when an agency "wrongfully withholds" agency records.

3. **Special FOIA definition of "agency":** The FOIA definition of "agency" includes entities that may not be subject to other APA requirements, such as

government corporations and executive branch entities that may collect information, but have no power to take actions having any legal effect.

B. Exceptions to FOIA

FOIA contains nine categories of exceptions to the requirement that agencies disclose their records. *See* 5 U.S.C. §552(b)(1)-(9). The Supreme Court has stated repeatedly that FOIA exemptions should be narrowly construed. The exceptions include classified national defense and foreign policy records; records concerning agency personnel matters; privileged or confidential business or financial records; trade secrets; privileged or confidential commercial information; law enforcement records where disclosure would harm law enforcement efforts; internal agency memoranda; personnel, medical, or law enforcement records where disclosure would unduly invade privacy; and records protected against disclosure by any other statute.

C. Disclosure of Exempt Records

Nothing in FOIA precludes an agency from voluntarily turning over records that FOIA exceptions would allow the agency to withhold. However, the Trade Secrets Act makes it a criminal offense for a government official to release information held to be within the FOIA trade-secrets exception. A person whose confidential information is threatened to be released by an agency has a "reverse-FOIA" cause of action under the APA's judicial review provisions (not the Trade Secrets Act itself) to prevent disclosure.

D. The Privacy Act of 1974

The Privacy Act of 1974, 5 U.S.C. §552a, prohibits agencies from disclosing records "except pursuant to a written request by, or with the prior consent of, the individual to whom the record pertains." The Privacy Act also restricts the information agencies are allowed to collect on individuals. The Privacy Act's nondisclosure provisions do not apply to records required to be disclosed under FOIA.

II. DISCOVERY FROM THE GOVERNMENT IN LITIGATION

The government has two special privileges that protect government records from discovery in litigation; evidentiary privilege and executive immunity (also known as executive privilege).

A. Evidentiary Privileges

Evidentiary privileges protect records in sensitive categories like state secrets, military secrets, and sensitive foreign affairs matters. The court determines whether the material sought in discovery is protected by a privilege by balancing the litigant's need for the information against the government's interest in secrecy.

B. Executive Immunity

When the executive branch claims immunity from the discovery process, the court balances the executive branch's need for confidentiality against the litigant's need for the material. When the President invokes executive privilege, the burden is on the party seeking discovery to demonstrate that the material is essential to justice.

III. OPEN-MEETINGS REQUIREMENTS

A. The Sunshine Act

In the Sunshine Act, 5 U.S.C. §552b, the government requires all agencies (using FOIA's definition of "agency") that are headed by a "collegial body composed of two or more individual members," to announce their meetings at least one week in advance and to open those meetings to the public, unless a Sunshine Act exception applies. Agencies headed by a single individual are not subject to the Sunshine Act, even when the head of the agency meets with subordinates to discuss agency business.

1. **"Meeting of an agency":** A gathering of agency members is a "meeting of an agency" within the Sunshine Act if the members "jointly conduct or dispose of agency business." The Sunshine Act does not apply to meetings that are purely consultative in character when the agency does not purport to conduct business.

2. **When may an agency meet in private?** The Sunshine Act contains ten categories of exceptions to its open-meetings requirement, most of which track the exceptions to FOIA's disclosure requirements. *See* 5 U.S.C. §552b(c)(1)-(8). A meeting may be closed pursuant to the Sunshine Act exceptions only by a public vote of a majority of the members of the agency.

B. The Federal Advisory Committee Act (FACA)

FACA requires presidential advisory committees, which include private citizens as members, to comply with the Sunshine Act with regard to their meetings and with FOIA with regard to their records. Because it interferes with the President's ability to seek advice from private citizens, it has been argued that FACA violates the separation of powers.

EXAM TIPS

EXAM TIPS

SUMMARY OF CONTENTS

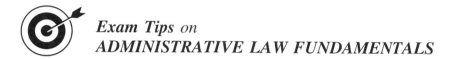

Exam Tips on
ADMINISTRATIVE LAW FUNDAMENTALS

Here are some important issues to keep in mind in connection with any administrative law exam:

Sources of law

☞ You should be clear on an exam about the ***source of the law*** that is relevant to the issues. Be explicit about when you are drawing on the ***Constitution***, the ***APA,*** the ***particular agency's statute,*** some ***other statute*** or ***traditional common-law*** principles.

☞ Whenever an issue arises regarding agency power to act, look carefully at and draw upon the agency's ***enabling act.***

Public choice and public interest theories

☞ The political background often helps understand agency action.

   ☞ If, under public choice theory, it appears that an agency was ***captured*** by a powerful interest group, you might express skepticism about the agency's actions.

   ☞ On the other hand, if it appears agency experts are pursuing an important ***public policy goal,*** you might argue for deference to the agency.

Exam Tips on
SEPARATION OF POWERS AND DISTRIBUTION OF ADMINISTRATIVE POWER

Nondelegation

☞ In nondelegation doctrine issues, it often is useful to address the history of the doctrine and explain how it has evolved from a strict, categorical approach to the current intelligible principle standard.

   ☞ Point out that the nondelegation doctrine is a very lenient standard and that no statute has failed the intelligible principle test in recent years. Mention the *Whitman* case as the most recent example.

   ☞ If a question calls for an extended discussion of the nondelegation doctrine, it is helpful to ground that discussion in Justice Rehnquist's analysis in his *Benzene* concurrence of the normative bases for the doctrine, most importantly that Congress makes the basic policy choices.

   ☞ It also may be useful to discuss the nondelegation doctrine in light of larger separation of powers concerns such as those raised in Justice Scalia's *Mistretta* dissent.

Separation of powers

☞ In all separation of powers questions, start the discussion by identifying and applying any relevant constitutional provisions, such as the bicameralism and presentment clauses with regard to the legislative veto or the Appointments Clause in appointment and removal cases. Then go on to discuss more general separation of powers concerns that arise in cases involving issues such as the legislative veto, appointment and removal powers, presidential control and the like.

Appointment and removal

☞ In many appointment and removal cases, it is important to understand the remedy — the Court usually prohibits an official from exercising a power instead of holding that the method of appointment or removal was unconstitutional.

☞ For example, point out that any official appointed by or removable by Congress cannot exercise powers reserved to "officers of the United States" since "officers of the United States" only may be appointed in accordance with the Appointments Clause and may not be removed by Congress.

☞ If relevant, mention that Congress may appoint and remove its own officials.

☞ In cases involving Congress's power to restrict the President's power to remove executive officials, be sure to analyze the issue in light of Congress's broad power to restrict removal that the Court recognized in *Morrison v. Olson.* While a discussion of the "quasi-legislative" and "quasi-judicial" language of *Humphrey's Executor* might be appropriate, *Morrison* better represents current law.

Constitutionality of agency adjudication

☞ When discussing the constitutionality of locating adjudication within administrative agencies, be sure to explore the different treatment accorded public rights and private rights and be sure to analyze the issue in light of the factors stated in *CFTC v. Schor,* including that the agency adjudication occurs in a particularized area of law related to a regulatory scheme, that orders are enforceable only in court, that effective judicial review is available, and that the essence of the judicial power is not delegated to the agency.

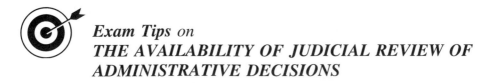

Exam Tips on
THE AVAILABILITY OF JUDICIAL REVIEW OF ADMINISTRATIVE DECISIONS

Jurisdiction vs. reviewability

☞ Be sure to keep the issues of jurisdiction and reviewability separate. You are more likely to be asked about reviewability than about jurisdiction.

☞ If jurisdiction is an issue, mention the old "rule of thumb" and then explain that jurisdiction depends mainly on what court has jurisdiction by statute.

☞ Point out that the Supreme Court favors jurisdiction in the court of appeals for reasons of judicial economy and thus if there is a statute that can be construed to give jurisdiction to that court, the Supreme Court will probably read it to do so.

General reviewability issues

☛ When discussing whether an agency action is reviewable, be sure to discuss whether the action is final, whether there are any ripeness problems, and whether either of the sections of APA §701 (a) affect reviewability.

☞ However, if the action is obviously reviewable, don't waste time discussing reviewability in depth — it is probably not being asked about.

Statutory preclusion of review

☛ For statutory preclusion of review, be sure to look for both explicit and implicit preclusion.

☛ If there is statutory preclusion, be sure to evaluate whether the particular action over which review is sought is within the scope of the precluding statute.

☞ If the statute precludes review of particular decisions such as a denial of government benefits, analyze whether the party seeking judicial review is challenging the type of decision specified in the statute or whether the party seeking judicial review is challenging something else, such as the way the entire program is being administered.

☞ In cases involving global challenges to the way an entire program is being administered, point out that the Court, in the *McNary* decision, seems open to arguments that global challenges are not precluded by statutes disallowing review of individual denials of benefits.

Committed to agency discretion by law

☛ In evaluating whether an action is committed to agency discretion by law, be sure to look for all three ways in which that can happen; no law to apply, a deeming clause, and a category traditionally not subject to judicial review.

☛ Make clear that these three understandings are related, that each tend to support the other, and that all involve evidence that Congress did not intend to subject the agency action to review.

☛ Look for arguments that the challenged agency action is akin to prosecutorial discretion. If it is, analyze reviewability under that line of cases.

☛ Remember that there is serious doubt about whether review of constitutional issues may be barred.

Standing

☛ Be sure the party seeking to challenge agency action has standing. Look for injury, causation, redressability, zone of interests, and the prudential limitations. Since the precedent in this area appears inconsistent, marshal arguments from both sides to show that you understand the issues even if the conclusion is not obvious.

☛ When the party seeking to challenge agency action is not the regulated party, be sure to discuss the zone of interests test and how it differs from the legal rights test.

☞ If there is a citizen suit provision, point out that everyone given permission to sue under that provision is probably within the zone of interests.

☞ In cases arising under statutes other than the APA, point out that the zone of interests test might not apply, since the zone of interests test may be based on the language of APA §702.

☛ Also, look for redressability problems — will the court be able to provide an effective remedy?

☛ The prudential limitations, including the ban on asserting the rights of third parties and the ban on litigating a generalized grievance, are subject to repeal by Congress.

☞ Look for repeal, such as by a citizen suit provision.

☞ Remember, however, that Congress may not override constitutional standing doctrines.

Ripeness and exhaustion

☛ Ripeness questions often arise when it appears that the agency's consideration is not complete. A common ripeness issue is whether a court should review a regulation before the agency has tried to enforce it. Use the *Abbott Labs* **fitness** and **hardship** tests. The differences between *Abbott Labs* and the *Toilet Goods* case are useful in applying the fitness and hardship test.

☛ An attempt to force an agency to act may raise ripeness questions. If you are asked whether an agency can be compelled to act, be sure to address whether the agency's failure to act is ripe.

☞ Agency inaction, as in a refusal to act, may not be ripe for review if the agency is still deciding whether to act although there may be a factual argument that the agency has delayed so long that its delay amounts to a decision not to act.

☛ If exhaustion of administrative remedies is an issue, apply the factors from the *McCarthy* opinion. However if agency action is final under the APA, those factors may not apply and the only issue may be whether a statute or regulation requires that certain remedies be exhausted.

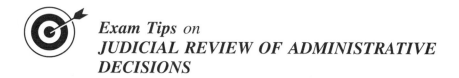

Exam Tips on
JUDICIAL REVIEW OF ADMINISTRATIVE DECISIONS

Standards of review

☛ Always look carefully at APA §706 to determine which standard of review applies to the particular agency action challenged.

Substantial evidence and de novo review

☞ If the predicates for substantial evidence review (agency decision under formal procedures or "on the record after hearing") are present, substantial evidence review applies. In a close case, it might be useful to spend time analyzing whether substantial evidence review applies.

☞ De novo review is rarely available and not likely to be tested on. However, if it appears that a predicate for de novo review is present, be sure to state the grounds — where agency adjudicatory factfinding procedures are inadequate and where new factual issues arise in an action to enforce non-adjudicatory agency action — and be sure to explain that under de novo review, the reviewing court makes a fresh determination of the facts subject to de novo review.

☞ If no predicate for either substantial evidence review or de novo review is present, use the arbitrary and capricious test, and explain that this test always applies since it has no predicate.

☛ When applying any standard of review, remember that under APA §706, the court looks at the ***whole record,*** not just those parts of the record that support the agency. Thus, if an exam calls for review of a particular agency action, be sure to address the complete record.

☛ The substantial evidence test applies to formal adjudication and formal rulemaking done under §§556 and 557 or otherwise "on the record after hearing."

☞ Point out that except where §§556 and 557 are specified, courts rarely find that substantial evidence review applies — the hearing must truly be "on the record" in the sense of a formal adjudicatory-type hearing.

☞ If the substantial evidence test applies, state the definition of the test ("such relevant evidence as a reasonable mind might accept as adequate to support a conclusion") and be sure to look at the whole record and discuss whether the evidence against the agency's decision substantially outweighs the evidence on the other side.

Issues of law: *Chevron*

☛ On issues of law, remember that there are competing traditions.

☞ If the issue is one of pure statutory interpretation, apply the two-step *Chevron* standard and be sure to describe the more and less deferential versions of step one.

☞ Unless the question really calls for it, don't spend too much time on step two.

☞ If the issue is not a pure question of statutory interpretation, it may be an application of law to a particular situation, which gets deferential, "reasonable basis and warrant in the record," review.

☛ Watch for situations in which *Chevron* does not apply because of the informality of the agency process leading to the interpretation. With informal interpretations, apply *Skidmore* deference.

Arbitrary and capricious

☛ On issues subject to arbitrary and capricious review, be sure to state the standard as laid down in *Overton Park* and then apply the test to the issues at hand.

☞ Be sure that the agency applied the correct legal standard, considered all relevant factors, considered alternatives, and explained its decision adequately, which includes stating conclusions on the major issues raised.

☛ When grounds for setting aside agency action exist, discuss the appropriate remedy — should the court remand the issue to the agency for further consideration, should the court allow the agency to supplement the record, or should the court simply rule that the agency may not do what it proposes?

Exam Tips on AGENCY CHOICE OF POLICYMAKING MODE

Rulemaking vs. adjudication

☛ As is the case in many areas in administrative law, look for relevant APA sections first, and make sure to apply them to the exam question.

☞ Recall that the APA does not clearly state when agencies must use one process or another, so in a question regarding the choice between rulemaking and adjudication, stress the discretionary nature of the decision.

☞ Consult the definitions in APA §551, but be sure to point out that courts have not found them to be binding.

☛ In questions involving whether due process requires a hearing, be sure to discuss whether the administrative action affects a small number of parties based on their special characteristics.

☞ The discussion here would benefit from pointing out the distinction between legislative and adjudicative facts. It is often useful to discuss whether the hypothetical is more like *Londoner* or *Bi-Metallic*.

☞ If the agency finding is based on adjudicative facts, perhaps adjudication is required.

☞ If the agency finding is based on legislative facts, a rulemaking process may be sufficient.

☞ In discussing whether an agency has power to use rulemaking, extol the policy virtues of rulemaking, since those virtues seem important when courts broadly construe grants of rulemaking authority.

☞ On the other side, discuss how rulemaking may detract from a party's right to a hearing and how rulemaking may be contrary to Congress's intent for primarily adjudicatory agencies.

☞ For issues regarding agency authority to make policy through adjudication, stress that this is a longstanding practice among agencies and is traditionally part of the common-law adjudicatory process. If *Wyman-Gordon* is relevant, state the views of both opinions in favor of the judgment since no view captured a majority.

Rulemaking exceptions

☞ If an agency makes a rule without notice and comment, look at the exceptions listed in APA §553 and go down the list to see if the agency's action falls within one of them.

☞ Discuss the question in light of the definition of a legislative rule. Be sure to point out that legislative rules create binding law while non-legislative rules do not.

Agency decisions without a formal process

☞ If an agency makes a decision with no formal process, look to the governing statute to see whether the agency was supposed to use an adjudicatory or legislative process. Also, be sure to point out any agency rules that require procedures in addition to those provided.

☞ If no such requirement appears to exist, mention the APA requirement of providing an answer and a statement of reasons. Also, point out that if an agency does not use a formal process, any norm created cannot be considered binding law.

Exam Tips on
APA RULEMAKING PROCEDURES

APA and rulemaking

☞ The starting place for all discussions of rulemaking procedure should be the APA.

☞ For example, if you are asked a notice question, start with the language of §553's notice requirement and then move on to the major cases construing that requirement.

Bias and ex parte contacts

☞ In controversies regarding bias and ex parte contacts, it is useful to point out that the APA does not address these issues with regard to informal rulemaking. Compare and contrast the various courts' approaches to the issues and then return to the APA and discuss whether one approach is more faithful to the APA.

Rulemaking procedures

☞ When answering questions regarding potential procedural defects in a rulemaking, in addition to the APA, support your analysis with the policies underlying the rulemaking process.

   ☞ For example, in notice controversies, discuss whether the purpose of notice — providing interested parties a genuine opportunity to participate — is met or not.

   ☞ In controversies regarding ex parte contacts and biased decisionmakers, in addition to discussing the adequacy of the opportunity to participate, discuss the tension between rulemaking on a legal model and rulemaking as part of the political system.

Vermont Yankee

☞ If a party claims that an agency should have used more than §553 procedures in a rulemaking, look to see whether any statute or rule required more. If not, *Vermont Yankee* counsels against requiring more than §553.

☞ *Vermont Yankee* can be raised in all questions regarding procedural issues in rulemaking.

   ☞ *Vermont Yankee*'s policies of predictability and procedural flexibility are implicated whenever a court is asked to read a provision of §553 broadly. It is thus effective to use *Vermont Yankee* as an argument against any but the most literal reading of the language of §553.

   ☞ If the question raises an issue regarding whether an agency conducting informal rulemaking might be required to go beyond the procedures specified in §553, *Vermont Yankee* must be addressed.

Formal rulemaking

☞ In a question regarding whether an agency is required to use formal rulemaking procedures, it is important to note that the Supreme Court favors the more streamlined informal rulemaking process.

   ☞ Be sure to point to the language of §553 and the particular agency's statute and argue that unless the statute clearly requires a hearing and an "on the record" decision, formal rulemaking is not required.

Exam Tips on
AGENCY ADJUDICATION AND DUE PROCESS

Public rights vs. private rights

☛ In any problem regarding the constitutionality of administrative adjudication, watch for the private rights issue.

 ☞ Pay attention to whether the right being adjudicated is within the core of Article III or whether it is arguable that the adjudication at issue is in a category normally thought to be appropriate for a non–Article III tribunal.

 ☞ It also may be helpful to contrast Justice Brennan's categorical approach with the majority's approach under which a much looser separation of powers standard applies.

Property and liberty interests

☛ In due process cases, it is important to address first whether there is a protected interest, usually either property or liberty.

 ☞ If the question involves property, clearly identify the source of any protected entitlement. Be creative and go beyond the bare words of state law when there is an argument for an implicit interest under *Perry v. Sindermann.*

 ☞ In liberty cases, distinguish between "entitlement liberty" and "constitutional liberty."

  ☞ In a constitutional liberty case, identify the nature of the protected liberty interest.

  ☞ In an entitlement liberty case, identify the source and nature of the protected liberty interest.

What process is due?

☛ When deciding what process is due, analyze each element of the *Mathews v. Eldridge* test separately.

 ☞ When applying the third element, look for indications that less procedure is desirable for reasons other than the state's pure desire to save time and resources on procedure, e.g., perhaps because an emergency necessitates quick action.

 ☞ In employment cases, note that the Supreme Court has decided categorically that due process requires at least an informal pre-termination oral hearing.

 ☞ In other areas, note that the Court has allowed for paper procedures pretermination except when subsistence benefits are concerned, as in *Goldberg v. Kelly.*

☞ Be sure to note that in most situations when a pretermination oral hearing is not required, such a hearing must be provided posttermination.

Bias vs. prejudgment

☛ Be clear about the difference between bias and prejudgment, and discuss explicitly the facts that lead to an argument that one or the other is present.

Statutory right to a hearing

☛ In cases involving the statutory right to a hearing, identify the source of the right to a hearing. Look explicitly into whether statutes or regulations limit the scope of the hearing.

☞ If there is a due process issue regarding a substantive limitation on the scope of a hearing, the irrebuttable presumption doctrine may be relevant in reinforcing the general rule that the scope of the hearing is tailored to the substantive issues as specified in the statute and regulations. However, it is important to note that the irrebuttable presumption doctrine is no longer good law.

Exam Tips on
SUBSTANTIVE POLICYMAKING IN AGENCIES

☛ The material in this chapter can be used to supplement exam discussion of substantive standards on judicial review.

☞ For example, on questions regarding substantive standards of review, discussion of reasoned decisionmaking and clarity and consistency requirements could supplement discussion of APA §706's arbitrary and capricious or substantial evidence standards of review.

Cost-benefit analysis

☛ In questions raising issues regarding cost-benefit analysis, the starting point should be the agency's statute — does it clearly require cost-benefit analysis? If not, then cost-benefit analysis is probably not required.

☞ A discussion of the strengths and weaknesses of cost-benefit analysis could supplement an answer raising cost-benefit issues.

☛ If an exam has a question in which an agency conducts a cost-benefit analysis, it might be useful to look at the agency's statute to determine whether the agency is allowed to do cost-benefit analysis or whether a statutory provision precludes it.

National Environmental Policy Act

☛ The most likely questions regarding NEPA concern the contents of the EIS and what the agency must do with the EIS once it is prepared.

☞ In the latter regard, it may be helpful to explain the value of a purely procedural NEPA.

☞ Be sure also to explain your answer in light of the text of NEPA, which provides only that the EIS must be prepared and must "accompany" the agency's proposal through all review stages.

Post-decision support

☛ Watch for agency arguments in support of agency action on grounds that were not relied upon at the agency level and point out that agency action must stand or fall on the grounds the agency relied upon when it made its decision.

Clarity requirements

☛ In a question that raises clarity concerns, point out that the cases imposing clarity requirements on due process grounds may be out of date or inconsistent with the *Roth* line of cases regarding property interests.

☞ Further, it is unclear whether, as a nonconstitutional matter, the APA imposes a similar requirement on federal agencies. It can be argued, however, that absent a clear standard, agency action is arbitrary.

Estoppel and nonacquiescence

☛ In a question raising the issue of whether the representations of an official can estop the agency, state the general rule that agencies are not estopped by such conduct. Point out that for constitutional reasons, the rule is even stronger when expenditure of funds is involved.

☛ In a question raising issues of collateral estoppel and agency nonacquiescence, it may be useful to explain why agencies may wish to adhere to their views without necessarily appealing every adverse ruling.

☞ It is clear that nonmutual collateral estoppel does not apply against the government in litigation.

☞ However, within a circuit that has rejected the agency's view, the rule of law may require the agency to acquiesce to the court's ruling.

Exam Tips *on*
AGENCY ENFORCEMENT AND LICENSING

Prosecutorial discretion

☛ In questions about prosecutorial discretion, reviewability issues are likely to be very important.

☞ Argue that exercises of prosecutorial discretion are presumptively unreviewable.

☞ Then, look for any indication that the agency's statute restricts or compels prosecutions under certain circumstances to rebut the presumption of unreviewability.

Discriminatory enforcement

☛ In questions raising claims of discriminatory enforcement, apply the "patent abuse of discretion" standard to claims of discriminatory enforcement, and discuss how difficult courts have made it to prevail on such claims.

Occupational and business licensing

☛ Occupational and business licensing exam questions are most likely to raise due process property interest questions.

☞ Analyze the particular scheme under *Roth* and then look for special problems such as capture of the licensing body by a segment of the profession or industry looking to avoid competition from another segment.

☞ If capture appears to be present, discuss whether *Gibson v. Berryhill* or *Friedman v. Rogers* should govern. Recall that under *Friedman v. Rogers,* the *Gibson* rule may not extend beyond the context of disciplinary hearings.

FCC licensing

☛ In FCC licensing questions, watch for questions raising *Ashbacker* and *Storer* issues.

☞ On *Storer* issues, watch for an argument by the applicant that the FCC's rule should not apply in the particular case.

☞ Note that comparative hearings are now required only on initial licensing decisions and not on renewals.

Ratemaking

☛ Ratemaking is not a common area for examination, except perhaps as an example of important issues that apply across the administrative law spectrum.

☞ Due process hearing issues are important since ratemaking is often conducted in a formal hearing.

☞ In ratemaking questions, watch for *Morgan* issues, in which the decisionmaker does not actually hear the evidence or engages in ex parte communications with agency officials before deciding on the proper rate structure. If *Morgan* is relevant, point out that the later *Morgan* decisions make it difficult to police agency conduct in presiding over ratemaking proceedings.

Exam Tips on
AGENCY INFORMATION GATHERING

☞ The most likely candidates for examination from the material in this chapter include warrantless inspections and the requirements for obtaining warrants, drug testing of government employees, and the collective entity rule regarding Fifth Amendment rights against self-incrimination.

Inspections

☞ In a question raising an issue regarding an inspection, discuss first any doubts that the agency has the authority to conduct inspections.

☞ Then look to whether the agency had a warrant.

☞ If the agency had a warrant, the warrant may be subject to attack if the inspection was not part of the routine operation of a regulatory scheme.

☞ If the agency did not have a warrant, look to whether the search meets the requirements for warrantless searches of pervasively regulated businesses.

Drug testing

☞ In a question about drug testing, discuss whether the particular employee or employees that the government wants to test are in sensitive positions or have been involved in an incident justifying special scrutiny. Otherwise, the testing might not be proper.

Subpoena enforcement

☞ In a case involving production of documents or provision of information to the government, if it is relevant raise the collective entity rule and the rule that custodians of entity records may not raise Fifth Amendment objections to providing such records.

☞ It also is useful to note that courts do not like issues of agency authority to be litigated in the context of the enforcement of a subpoena.

☞ Finally, if a privilege such as the attorney-client privilege is raised, be sure to note that the applicability of state-law privileges to federal administrative proceedings has not been established.

Exam Tips on
PRIVATE ENFORCEMENT OF REGULATORY NORMS AND PREEMPTION

☞ The material in this chapter is rarely tested on because it is not central to most administrative law courses. The material on private rights of action may be tested on more often than the remainder of the material.

Citizens' suits

☞ In any question regarding citizens' suits, the language of the particular citizens' suit provision should be the starting place for analysis.

☞ On a question regarding the relationship between citizens' suit provisions and judicial review, the recent decision in *Bennett v. Spear* provides the framework for understanding.

☞ The important point is that citizens' suit provisions are narrow, allowing claims against the government only when the government fails to perform a nondiscretionary duty or violates the relevant statute as a regulated private party might violate it.

☞ Citizens' suits often raise standing issues.

☞ You should distinguish between prudential limits on standing, such as the zone of interests test, which citizens' suit provision can affect and constitutional standing requirements, which citizens' suit provisions cannot affect.

Implied private rights of action

☞ In a question about implied private rights of action, it may be useful to compare the current "intent of Congress" standard to the two standards that preceded it, the *J.I. Case* "advance the statutory purposes" standard and the four-factor test of *Cort v. Ash*.

Preemption

☞ On preemption questions, the starting point for analysis should be statutory language, including preemption provisions, partial preemption provisions, and savings clauses.

☞ If there is no express preemption provision, look for implied preemption through "field preemption," "actual conflict preemption," or "obstacle to the legislative purpose" preemption.

Judicial remedies and agency jurisdiction

☞ In a case involving overlap between judicial remedies and the jurisdiction of a federal agency, apply the primary jurisdiction doctrine.

☞ If it appears that the agency has jurisdiction over a dispute, and the dispute is within the expertise of the agency, then there is an argument that a judicial remedy should not be allowed until the agency has had the opportunity to address the case.

Exam Tips *on*
LIABILITY OF AGENCIES AND OFFICIALS

☞ The issues in this chapter are not often tested on, since they are not at the core of administrative law. However, FTCA issues are sometimes tested on, and some instructors may include minor issues on the liability matters addressed herein.

Federal Tort Claims Act

☞ In answering any FTCA question, look carefully at the statute and ask whether a statutory basis for liability exists and, if so, does an exception bar liability.

☞ In discussing the discretionary function exception, which is the FTCA issue most likely to be tested, it may be helpful to discuss the regulatory functions exception that the Court rejected.

    ☞ Be sure to spell out the governing test for the exception ("choice or judgment" and "the exercise of discretion in furtherance of public policy goals") and compare the official activity in the examination with the official activity in cases such as *Gaubert* and *Berkovitz.*

Liability of officials

☞ In a damages action against a government official, if the claim is a constitutional claim, the issue is whether a *Bivens* action is available.

    ☞ Regarding *Bivens* actions, look for remedies that Congress has declared as substitutes for *Bivens* or for special factors counseling hesitation.

    ☞ Be aware that even if Congress has not specified that an alternate remedy is a substitute for *Bivens,* it may displace the *Bivens* remedy as a special factor.

☞ With regard to official liability for damages under either *Bivens* or §1983, apply the functional approach to determine whether the official should receive absolute immunity.

    ☞ For officials entitled only to qualified immunity, remember that the subjective factor is no longer relevant, so that the official is liable only if he or she violated clearly established law.

Municipal liability

☞ With regard to municipal liability, watch for attempts to hold cities liable that are actually attempts to get around the ban on vicarious liability through some clever way of alleging a municipal policy or custom.

   ☞ The Court is very strict on requiring a municipal policy, and it thus does not make it easy to hold cities liable for constitutional violations committed by city employees.

   ☞ Thus, while claims for inadequate training or screening of employees exist in theory, you should be clear that such claims are very difficult to win because they are too close to vicarious liability.

Exam Tips on
FREEDOM OF INFORMATION AND OPEN MEETINGS

☞ The most likely area in this chapter to be tested on is FOIA.

   ☞ Likely questions include those asking about the coverage of FOIA (what are agency records?) and about FOIA exemptions.

☞ The other candidate for examination is the Government in the Sunshine Act, with questions focusing on what constitutes a meeting of an agency and whether an exception to the Sunshine Act allows for a private meeting.

Standing

☞ Standing questions also might come up in terms of who has standing to raise a FOIA or Sunshine Act issue in litigation and who has standing to try to prevent an agency from disclosing information in response to a FOIA request.

Freedom of Information Act

☞ In a question about FOIA, be sure to cite and quote from the statutory provision at issue.

   ☞ Be prepared to discuss whether particular information is contained in agency records.

   ☞ Watch out for records that are not in the agency's possession and were not in the agency's possession at the time of the FOIA request.

☞ Regarding FOIA exemptions, be sure to quote the statutory provision and keep in mind that courts construe the exemptions narrowly.

   ☞ Keep in mind that more than one exemption may arguably apply to a particular agency record, and be sure to discuss all exemptions that might apply.

☛ In a case in which a party supplying information to the agency seeks to prevent the agency from providing records in response to a third party's FOIA request, discuss the issue in terms of the requirements for "reverse FOIA" actions.

    ☞ Point out that the APA provides judicial review of an agency decision to release information, and that other statutes, such as the Trade Secrets Act and the Privacy Act, may provide a legal basis for reversing the agency on judicial review.

☛ Privacy-based FOIA exemptions are likely to be asked about. Be sure to discuss the balancing test used to determine whether the public's need to know is outweighed by a potential invasion of privacy.

Discovery against the government

☛ On any question regarding discovery from the government in litigation, be sure to point out that the government may not only resist discovery on all the grounds that other parties may employ, but also may raise evidentiary privileges and executive immunity.

    ☞ In either case, the procedure for raising the objection, including whether the material is presumed to be available in discovery or presumed to be confidential, may be relevant.

Sunshine Act

☛ In questions about the Sunshine Act, be sure to consider whether an agency meeting is involved and whether the particular agency is covered by the Act.

    ☞ If an agency meeting is involved, and an agency wishes to hold it in private, look both at the substance of the Sunshine Act's exceptions and whether the agency has followed proper procedures for closing a meeting.

SHORT-ANSWER
QUESTIONS
AND
ANSWERS

SHORT-ANSWER QUESTIONS

ADMINISTRATIVE LAW FUNDAMENTALS

1. Is administrative law, especially administrative procedure, derived solely from the APA? _____

2. What functions do administrative agencies fulfill? _____

3. What are the differences between public interest and public choice theories of agency action? _____

CHAPTER 2

SEPARATION OF POWERS AND DISTRIBUTION OF ADMINISTRATIVE POWER

4. Congress enacts a statute authorizing the President to grant favorable trade status to a foreign nation on a finding that the foreign nation "meets acceptable standards on human rights" or that favorable trade status is "in the best interests of the United States." Would this statute violate the nondelegation doctrine? _____

5. An amendment to the Internal Revenue Code provides that the Internal Revenue Service (IRS) must submit all proposed regulations to the House Ways and Means Committee. If the committee is silent, the regulations go into effect sixty days after submission. If the committee (by majority vote) disapproves of a regulation, then the effective date of the regulation is delayed a further 120 days to allow time to introduce (and possibly pass) a bill disapproving the regulation. Normal procedures regarding presentment to the President, veto, and override apply to this bill. If a disapproval bill does not become law within

the 120 days, the regulation goes into effect. Is this a constitutional method of oversight? _____

6. Congress passes a statute stating that the President must have good cause before firing United States attorneys and that the Senate may, by a majority vote, reject presidential removal of United States attorneys. Are these restrictions constitutional? _____

7. Congress is upset about the way that the President is distributing highway funds, so in its new appropriations bill it provides that the comptroller general has the power to reject allocations of highway funds made by the Secretary of Transportation. Is this provision constitutional? _____

8. Congress is upset with the President's choices for United States attorneys, so it passes (over veto) a statute delegating the authority to appoint United States attorneys to the courts of appeals, each of which would appoint the United States attorneys for districts within their respective circuits. Is that constitutional? _____

9. The Federal Emergency Management Agency (FEMA) in the Department of Homeland Security (DHS) needs to hire more claims officers to process claims for disaster relief in the wake of disasters. Claims officers counsel disaster victims on which claims to file and how to file them. They also receive the claims and forward them, with a recommendation, to claims adjusters, who have authority to grant or deny claims. Congress specifies by statute that the Director of FEMA, not the Secretary of DHS, "shall have the authority to hire claims officers." Is this a constitutional appointments process? _____

10. **True or false with explanation:** The Line Item Veto Act would have been constitutional had it been incorporated by explicit reference into subsequent appropriations and tax relief bills, but only with regard to the appropriations and limited tax benefits contained in those particular bills. _____

11. **True or false with explanation:** As long as an official performs quasi-legislative or quasi-judicial functions, Congress may participate in the appointment of that official and it may restrict the President's removal of that official. _____

12. Could Congress delegate the authority to establish income tax rates to the Secretary of the Treasury? _____

CHAPTER 3

THE AVAILABILITY OF JUDICIAL REVIEW OF ADMINISTRATIVE DECISIONS

13. Does the existence of federal question jurisdiction, without an amount in controversy requirement, mean that judicial review is available for all agency action? _____

14. Assume Congress enacts a food stamp program that provides for three categories of food stamp assistance: emergency assistance, interim assistance, and regular assistance.

Emergency assistance is provided on the day of an application when the applicant establishes, to the satisfaction of a caseworker, that the applicant is in dire need of assistance. Interim assistance is provided within ten days of an application for regular assistance when a caseworker concludes that it is likely that the agency will grant the application for regular assistance. Regular assistance is granted when, after full review, eligibility is established under program guidelines. The statute grants judicial review of denials of interim and regular assistance. The statute does not mention review of denials of emergency assistance. Are denials of emergency assistance reviewable? _____

15. Assume the same situation as above except that Congress has provided for review of denials of emergency and regular benefits but not interim benefits. How would the arguments against reviewability differ? _____

16. Regarding the same food stamp program, suppose a person files for emergency assistance and then after a week has still not received an answer. Can the applicant obtain judicial review of the failure to answer? _____

17. A statute provides that "the Administrator of the Environmental Protection Agency shall, in his discretion, designate those toxic waste sites that shall be given priority treatment" under the laws regulating the cleanup of toxic wastes. Priority treatment means that the site is cleaned up immediately, while normally the EPA delays cleanup while it tries to assign responsibility and recover cleanup costs in advance. A group of neighbors (near a particularly bad toxic waste site) sue the administrator when the administrator decides not to designate the site for priority treatment. Is the administrator's action subject to judicial review? _____

18. What would be the proper response to a petition for review filed against the Administrator of OSHA alleging that "the Administrator has failed to take adequate steps to ensure that all Americans work in a safe and healthful environment as required by statute"?

_____

19. AT&T is upset that the FCC is giving favorable treatment to MCI and Sprint regarding rate regulation and the tariff-filing requirement. AT&T wants to sue the FCC. Would AT&T have standing to sue? _____

20. In order to receive federal funds under the Aid to Families with Dependent Children program (AFDC), states are required to take action to establish paternity and to secure child support orders from noncustodial parents (usually fathers) of children receiving AFDC benefits. Child support orders usually exceed the amount of AFDC benefits that are provided in the absence of a child support order. Further, without a paternity determination, a child cannot inherit from the estate of a noncustodial father. Does a child have standing to sue the state over the state's failure to attempt to establish paternity and the state's failure to seek a child support order against the child's noncustodial father? _____

21. A new regulation requires cigarette makers to disclose the ingredients of cigarettes on the package. The penalty for noncompliance is a substantial fine and seizure of all cigarettes in commerce not containing the proper labeling. Can the cigarette makers get immediate judicial review of this regulation upon its promulgation? _____

22. What are the different meanings of "committed to agency discretion by law"? What evidence should a court look for to determine whether a matter is "committed to agency discretion by law"? _____

23. Does a grocery store owner have standing to challenge the legality of the cutoff of food stamps to her customers? Would your answer change if you learned that an interest group representing shopkeepers lobbied heavily for passage of the food stamp statute and that the legislative history mentions the preservation of food stores in low-income neighborhoods as a positive "side effect" of the food stamp program? _____

CHAPTER 4

JUDICIAL REVIEW OF ADMINISTRATIVE DECISIONS

24. The Department of Agriculture decided to create a new method of regulating milk prices. Wanting the widest possible input, it decides to hold public hearings in eight locations around the country. The Secretary of Agriculture and other department officials were present at all eight hearings. The hearings were open to the public, and all attendees were allowed to address comments to and ask questions of the Secretary and the other officials present. After the rule was promulgated under APA §553, a milk producer from Wisconsin challenged the rule as not supported by substantial evidence. Is substantial evidence the proper standard for judicial review? _____

25. Does the arbitrary or capricious standard always apply? _____

26. The Bureau of Land Management approves a plan to harvest timber on ten thousand acres of federal land. This decision was made informally (there was no rulemaking or adjudication), and the decision was explained in a press release issued by the director of the Bureau. The decision is challenged on judicial review under the arbitrary and capricious test, and the Bureau asks the court to affirm its decision based exclusively upon affidavits from the Director and her assistants regarding the basis of the decision. Is this the proper procedure? _____

27. On review of the denial of a social security disability benefits claim, the agency argues that its doctor's testimony that the claimant was not disabled provides (on its own) substantial evidence to support the claim, and therefore the court need look no further into the record. Is this a good argument? _____

28. In determining the amount of food stamps to which a claimant is entitled, the statute requires the Department of Agriculture to consider "the resources available to the family unit." The department has recently decided, in a §553 rulemaking, to change its definition of "family unit" and place children who are unrelated (e.g., stepchildren) in the same "family unit," thus reducing benefits to the stepsiblings of children who are receiving child support payments. A claimant, whose claim was denied based on child support payments to a stepsibling, sues claiming that the statute does not allow stepsiblings to be included in the same "family unit." What is the standard of review for the definition of "family unit?" _____

29. In response to revelations that airbags have killed and injured children and smaller adults, the National Highway Transportation and Safety Administration (NHTSA) decides, in a §553 rulemaking, to rescind the regulation requiring dual airbags in all cars. It also allows those cars already manufactured with dual airbags to be equipped with on/off switches. The automobile insurers submitted comments, supported by scientific research, urging the retention of the airbag rule. They argued that redesigned airbags that did not deploy with so much force, combined with adjustments to the design of automobile dashboards, would resolve the problem. In its concise general statement, the agency did not mention the comments submitted by the insurers. Are the rescission of the airbags rule and the adoption of the switch requirement, arbitrary and capricious? _____

CHAPTER 5

AGENCY CHOICE OF POLICYMAKING MODE

30. A local zoning board decides, at a public legislative meeting, to increase the required side yard requirement for all homes built in the town, from six feet to ten feet. This decision was made based on a perception that, in areas of the town where the homes are closer than ten feet from the side property line, the lots look too crowded and property values might be harmed. The board also decides that in areas of special concern for open space, it will require twenty feet. At the meeting, the board members took a map of the town and designated twelve parcels of the approximately one thousand in the town as "special concern for open space," and thus required a twenty-foot side yard for any new development. Do any of the town's property owners have a due process claim against the changes in the side yard requirements? _____

31. A statute prohibits "unfair practices in the sale or leasing of automobiles." The statute creates an agency and gives the agency the power to enforce the statute through an elaborate adjudicatory process. The statute also gives the agency the power "to make rules to carry out the substantive provisions of the statute." Does this agency have the power to make a regulation specifying that turning back the odometer of an automobile is prohibited by the statute? Can the agency then use the regulation to limit the hearing to the issue of whether the automobile seller turned back the odometer? _____

32. Suppose the agency in the above question announces the odometer rule in an opinion deciding an individual adjudication of an alleged violation of the statute, and then applies the rule in subsequent adjudications under the Act. Should the agency be required to make the rule in a rulemaking as opposed to announcing it while deciding an individual adjudication? _____

33. A federal statute requires that dealers in dangerous wild animals, such as lions and tigers, have fences around the perimeter of their compounds that are "of sufficient structural strength to contain the animals in the event they escape their primary enclosures." For years, the agency in charge had approved fences of heights six feet and higher. Then the agency issued, without notice and comment, an interpretative ruling stating that such fences must be at least eight feet tall. The agency then began revoking the licenses of dealers with fences shorter than eight feet. Is this a proper interpretative rule? _____

34. A statute grants the Secretary of Agriculture the power to move agricultural programs from one Department of Agriculture facility to another. After internal study (with no public process whatsoever) the Secretary decides to move a very large research program about corn growing, from Wisconsin to Iowa. Should the Secretary have conducted a rulemaking or adjudication? _____

CHAPTER 6

APA RULEMAKING PROCEDURES

35. The EPA has evidence that gasoline fumes pose a serious air quality problem. The agency issues a Notice of Proposed Rulemaking (NPRM) that identifies the problem and includes the text of a proposed rule that would require a new gas tank assembly on all automobiles. The new gas tank assembly would reduce the fumes that escape during fueling and whenever the gas cap is taken off. Comments from automobile manufacturers and consumer groups convince the EPA that it would be cheaper to require the addition of a chemical to gasoline that would reduce the fumes emitted. May the EPA promulgate a regulation requiring the reformulation of gasoline without issuing a new NPRM? _____

36. On the same fact situation, assume that officials from General Motors attended a meeting with the Administrator of the EPA during the comment period. At the meeting, the attendees discussed the negative economic effects that would occur if the car makers were required to modify their gas tanks. Does this provide a basis for challenging the final rule? _____

37. Assume that the FDA issues a NPRM that proposes a label on all tobacco products stating "Tobacco is a Deadly Poison; Quit Now and Save Your Life." Suppose that evidence surfaces that, in a personal letter to one of his former medical school classmates, the Administrator of the FDA (who has final decisionmaking authority on the rulemaking) wrote: "I view my mission in life as making business as difficult as possible for tobacco companies so I can save as many people as possible from the effects of tobacco. I will never waver from this mission." Does this provide an argument for disqualifying the Administrator? _____

38. Assume the same rulemaking on tobacco products. The manufacturers of smokeless tobacco submit studies showing that their products are far less dangerous than cigarettes. In fact, the studies show that lives would be saved if people were encouraged to switch from cigarettes to their products. Suppose that the Administrator imposes the requirement on all tobacco products. In his concise general statement he addresses the dangers of tobacco in general terms and does not mention the issues raised by the smokeless tobacco manufacturers. Are there grounds for attacking the result? _____

39. OSHA is conducting a rulemaking on safety issues regarding employees who work at computer terminals. There are conflicting OSHA studies on the health effects of exposure to radiation from computer monitors. Interests representing employees present reputable studies showing negative health effects and how a relatively inexpensive modification of computer monitors would help. Monitor manufacturers and interests representing employers present studies showing no negative health effects and that monitor modification would be very expensive and would not eliminate the kind of radiation that the opposing experts say is the problem. OSHA imposes the regulation preferred by employees. On judicial review, the court of appeals states that, given the state of the record, the rule is arbitrary and capricious absent an opportunity for each side to cross-examine the other's experts. Is this a proper ruling? _____

40. An agency's organic statute states that the agency, before issuing a rule, "must hold an oral hearing at which interested parties may present argument and evidence." Does this trigger formal rulemaking under APA §§556 and 557? _____

CHAPTER 7

AGENCY ADJUDICATION AND DUE PROCESS

41. Congress decides that NHTSA regulations and state product liability law are not adequate to deal with the problem of defective automobiles contributing to accidents. Therefore, it has passed a statute creating the Automobile Defect Liability Board, an agency within the Department of Transportation. Congress has granted the board authority to adjudicate claims against automobile manufacturers for damages arising out of defective design or manufacture and violations of federal automobile safety regulations. Only a plaintiff may choose to have the case heard by the board. If the plaintiff files a claim to be heard by the board, there is no provision for transferring the case back to a state or federal court, unless the board decides that it lacks jurisdiction over the case. The statute provides that "Board orders are enforceable by application to the District Court" and "judicial review of Board orders shall be had under Chapter 7 of the APA." In its first decision, the board ruled that the seats of a particular car were defectively manufactured and that they did not meet federal safety standards. The board awarded one million dollars in damages to the plaintiff, who was injured when the car seat came loose from the floor of the car in an accident. On judicial review, the automobile manufacturer argues that the board's jurisdiction is unconstitutional. Is it? _____

42. A state statute regulating the employment of guards in a state prison provides that:

> "Guards employed by the Department of Corrections are employees at will, and can be terminated whenever, in the sole discretion and judgment of the Director of the Department or her designate, termination will serve the best interests of the Department." Department regulations provide that "prior to terminating the employment of a Guard, the Director or her designate will, whenever possible, meet with the employee to discuss the reasons for the termination, and to offer suggestions for alternative employment opportunities."

Do prison guards have a property interest in continued employment? _____

43. A state statute provides as follows:

Section 1. Teachers in public elementary schools may not be fired without cause, which means substandard performance, misconduct on the job, or illegal or immoral conduct outside the workplace.

Section 2. Whether cause for firing exists shall be determined by the principal of the school in which the teacher teaches, with any hearing or other procedure in the sole discretion of the principal.

Is this statute consistent with due process? _____

44. A state statute provides that police officers may inflict serious bodily harm to subdue any person acting in a disorderly fashion. Mr. Smith has a reaction to a new prescription medication and begins to behave erratically while walking on a public street. The police inflict serious bodily harm while subduing him. When he brings a constitutional claim for damages, the defense argues that, given the state law, he was not deprived of a protected interest. Is this a good argument? _____

45. A new president pledges to appoint administrators who are willing to be tough and assess large fines against environmental violators. As part of the plan, the EPA (with presidential approval) adopts regulations allowing the EPA to retain 50 percent of all fines collected. The funds must be used to hire more prosecutors and administrative law judges in order to increase enforcement activity. A chemical manufacturer is prosecuted for violations of the Clean Water Act and is assessed a fine higher than any on record, but still within statutory limits. The manufacturer challenges the fairness of the procedure. What result?

_____

46. The FTC regulates unfair and deceptive trade practices. The FTC Act provides that the FTC has authority, after an adjudicatory hearing on the record, to order businesses to cease and desist from an "unfair and deceptive practice." The FTC conducts a rule-making and promulgates a rule declaring that "it is an unfair and deceptive practice to represent through advertising, labeling, or otherwise that a product contains a unit of weight, volume, or other unit of measure that has no fixed meaning." The FTC holds a cease and desist hearing over Bad Cereal Corporation's claim that its raisin bran cereal contains three scoops of raisins, since no scoop size is specified. At the hearing, the only issue is whether Bad Cereal makes the claim in its advertising or labeling. The FTC refuses to reopen the issue of whether the practice is unfair and deceptive. Bad Cereal argues that this violates its right to a hearing. What result?

_____

47. True or false with explanation: A preexpulsion hearing is not required to expel a student from a state university for academic deficiency. _____

48. Assume that the ALJs that decide claims for welfare under the program at issue in *Goldberg v. Kelly* work for the state welfare agency and are subject to yearly performance reviews that the agency head uses to award merit pay raises and promotions. Further, ALJs are subject to discipline by the agency head and may be fired "for good cause including malfeasance in office and neglect of duty." Does this arrangement violate the procedural rights of a welfare recipient in a hearing to terminate benefits?

_____

SUBSTANTIVE POLICYMAKING IN AGENCIES

49. An agency is required to make all regulations "reasonably necessary to accomplish the goal of safety in federally subsidized public housing." After a widely publicized fire in a housing project that killed several people in apartments where the smoke detector batteries had been removed, the agency proposes a regulation requiring that all such housing contain central, hard-wired fire alarm systems. An interest group of owners of subsidized housing presents a study in the comment period, showing that the requirement's costs would be substantially greater than the benefits in terms of total losses from fires. Is this study grounds for a court rejecting the agency's requirement on judicial review?

_____

50. An agency proposes to locate a large office building in the midst of a residential neighborhood. The residents are concerned about traffic and other changes in the character of the neighborhood that the office building would cause — including the fact that the government would take several neighborhood stores and a church by eminent domain to make room for the project. Must the agency address these matters in its EIS concerning the project? _____

51. Assume that the government includes the information discussed above in its EIS, and the agency decides to go ahead with the building. In its explanation of the decision, the agency acknowledges the substantial effects on the community but decides that, overall, the benefits justify incurring those costs. The agency also rejects proposals to reduce the size of the building on the ground that it would be less convenient for the agency to have offices in two different places. Do these facts present grounds for a court rejecting the project under NEPA? _____

52. A statute grants the President the power to order the Army Corps of Engineers to make emergency repairs to dams and levees after a disaster. Must the Corps address the environmental effects of the emergency repairs in an Environmental Impact Statement?

_____

53. An agency denies an application for welfare benefits on the ground that the applicant earns too much money to qualify. The applicant seeks judicial review, and in his petition he establishes conclusively that the agency erred in calculating his income. The agency responds by pointing out that, under agency regulations, the applicant was ineligible because he had filed prior false applications with the agency. What result?

_____

54. Assume that on remand of the above application for benefits, the agency denies the benefits on the ground that the applicant had previously filed false applications. The applicant shows on judicial review that in many prior cases, the agency had granted benefits to people who had previously filed false applications. Is this a reason for reversing the agency? _____

55. A benefits recipient is told by an agency official that his benefits will continue unless he earns more than eight thousand dollars in a year. He earns seven thousand dollars in a year.

The agency, relying upon valid statutory standards, terminates his benefits and informs him of the statutory one-year waiting period for reapplying. Is the erroneous advice he received any reason to invalidate the agency's action? _____

CHAPTER 9

AGENCY ENFORCEMENT AND LICENSING

56. A person living near a large factory is upset that the EPA has not stopped the factory from emitting illegal air pollution. Can the person compel the EPA to bring an enforcement action against the factory owners? _____

57. NHTSA is concerned about minivan safety. It brings a proceeding against one manufacturer to force it to recall its minivans and change the latches on the rear doors, which NHTSA claims may open in relatively low-impact accidents. The manufacturer claims that all minivan latches are the same and that another company's latches open even more easily than its own. Is this a valid defense? _____

58. A new governor appoints a new state Attorney Disciplinary Board composed exclusively of members of large law firms. One of the board's first actions is to announce that it intends to enforce a longstanding (but rarely enforced) ban on practicing law under a trade name. It then issues an immediate suspension notice to four lawyers practicing under the name "The Legal Clinic" and orders them to appear before the board for a hearing to determine whether the board should revoke or suspend their licenses to practice law, and whether an order should issue prohibiting them from practicing under a trade name. Are there any procedural problems with the board's actions? _____

59. The FCC announces that a new radio frequency is available in Chicago. Two applications are filed for the frequency — one by Michael Jordan and one by Rupert Murdoch. The FCC, without a hearing, awards the frequency to Michael Jordan and denies Murdoch's application on the ground that he already owns the maximum number of radio stations allowed under FCC rules. Murdoch protests that the FCC should have held a comparative hearing before awarding the license to Michael Jordan. Does Murdoch have a valid complaint? _____

60. The Secretary of Energy is presiding over a ratemaking proceeding regarding natural gas prices. After the close of the hearings, the Secretary asks the head of the agency within the department directly responsible for overseeing natural gas distribution for an analysis of the natural gas market, with recommendations on rates. Only the Secretary and his staff see this memorandum, and the Secretary adopts most of the rate recommendations contained in the memorandum. Does this procedure provide a basis for a challenge to the rates? _____

61. **True or false with explanation:** After *Heckler v. Chaney,* a federal court should never delay the enforcement of an otherwise valid order on the ground that a similar order should be issued against another regulated party. _____

AGENCY INFORMATION GATHERING

62. OSHA has regulatory authority over workplace safety. The recent resurgence of cigar smoking has OSHA concerned about the second-hand cigar smoke exposure of people who work in restaurants and bars where cigar smoking is allowed. An OSHA inspector arrives at a Chicago Butt and Brew Pub Restaurant (which is part of a national chain of restaurant-bars that promote themselves as cigar friendly) and informs the manager that he is there to collect air samples in various locations around the restaurant, including "employee-only" areas such as the employee restrooms and employee lounge where employees eat and take breaks. Can the manager refuse entry?

_____

63. In the last several years, Los Angeles has seen a substantial increase in the number of illnesses suffered by people who eat raw food in restaurants. The Los Angeles Board of Health decides to inspect, four times per year, all restaurants that serve sushi and all restaurants with salad bars. Any restaurant that is subject to a complaint of food poisoning should be inspected as soon as possible after the Board receives the complaint. The Board's regulations provide that any restaurant that impedes the inspector from carrying out an inspection shall automatically lose its license and be closed until it allows the inspection. A patron of Billy's Salad and Sushi Bar on Melrose Avenue in Los Angeles contracted a severe case of food poisoning after eating at Billy's. Billy refuses to allow the Board's inspector to enter without a warrant. Does Billy have the right to insist that the inspector obtain a warrant? _____

64. As part of welfare reform, the federal government requires that states, in order to monitor eligibility, conduct regular inspections of a randomly selected group of at least 5 percent of the recipients of food stamps and transitional aid to needy families with dependent children. May state inspectors make consent to such inspections a condition of continued aid? _____

65. May the government require that all prospective government employees undergo drug tests as a condition for securing government employment? _____

66. The president of an insolvent national bank testifies in Congress that he has been unable to locate records regarding a significant number of bad loans, and he blames a former bank employee for the disappearance of the records. Later, the Federal Deposit Insurance Corporation (FDIC), an agency that insures bank deposits, believes that the bank has the records and directs a subpoena to the president of the bank for the bank's records of the transactions. There is a potential for criminal liability of both the bank and the president regarding the transactions and of the president for perjury in his testimony before Congress. Can either the bank or the president resist complying with the subpoena on Fifth Amendment self-incrimination grounds?

_____

PRIVATE ENFORCEMENT OF REGULATORY NORMS AND PREEMPTION

67. A provision of the Clean Air Act grants a citizens' suit for an injunction against any person, including all government entities, who violates any provision of the Act. The statute also grants an action to compel the performance of a mandatory duty against the Administrator of the EPA. The EPA has issued regulations governing second-hand smoke which allow smoking in workplaces as long as sufficient ventilation is in place. The American Lung Association is upset that the EPA did not ban indoor smoking at all workplaces. Can it use the citizens' suit provisions to attempt to compel stronger regulation? _____

68. Assume the same citizens' suit provision and the same set of issues. Does the American Lung Association have standing to sue? _____

69. A federal statute prohibits gender discrimination at high schools receiving federal funds. The statute specifies that the penalty for failing to maintain equality in all programs is a reduction in federal funds, with a total cutoff if the discrimination continues after initial reductions in funding. The school maintains only one hockey team (a boys' team) and a girl tries out for the team. The coach tells her that the hockey program is not open to girls. She brings suit in federal court against the school district for an injunction to allow her to try out for the team and for damages. Her claim is based on a violation of the statute prohibiting discrimination in schools receiving federal funds. Is this a proper claim? _____

70. A farmer complies with all federal regulations regarding the use of pesticides and fertilizer on his fields. However, the runoff from those fields is causing damage to downstream property owners. For example, it is killing the fish in his neighbor's fishing pond. The affected neighbors sue under state law to have the farmer's use of his property declared a nuisance. They ask for damages and an injunction. Does federal law allow this state law claim to be pressed? _____

71. A worker is fired during a union organizing campaign, and she sues her employer in federal court for violating the National Labor Relations Act by firing her in retaliation for pro-union activities. Can the claim go forward in court? _____

CHAPTER 12

LIABILITY OF AGENCIES AND OFFICIALS

72. A naval officer is traveling to his home, which is located off of the naval base, in a vehicle owned by the Navy. The car is part of the Navy's aging fleet of automobiles provided to certain officers. The officer's car is struck head-on by a civilian drunk driver who went through a red light. The officer is seriously injured. He sues the United States Navy under the Federal Torts Claim Act, alleging that the Navy was negligent for not providing him with an automobile equipped with an airbag. Is this a viable FTCA claim?

_____

73. NHTSA is charged with developing federal safety standards for automobiles and ensuring that automobiles meet them. Under governing statutes, manufacturers of safety-related automobile parts are required to meet strict standards, and automobiles containing safety-related parts from unapproved manufacturers may not be sold. Global Motors Inc. manufactures a mini van that contains airbags from an unapproved manufacturer. NHTSA knows this but allows the car to be sold anyway. In fact, the manufacturer flunked NHTSA tests and therefore was not certified. May a person, injured when an airbag fails to deploy in an accident, sue the government under the FTCA for injuries due to the government's failure to enforce the statutory safety requirements? _____

74. A member of the FTC makes a speech in which she criticizes tobacco company executives for pushing deadly drugs on young people. In the speech she argues that tobacco executives should be shunned socially for their contribution to the health problems of the nation. She names the CEOs of the five largest companies, including John Smith. After he became CEO of a tobacco company, Smith ordered the toughest restrictions on company advertising in the industry to keep cigarette advertising away from children. He sues the FTC commissioner under several state law theories, including defamation, tortious interference with contract, and false light. What result? _____

75. USDA inspectors obtained a warrant and inspected an egg farm. The inspection revealed numerous violations of USDA and OSHA regulations, some of which affected the safety of the eggs and some of which affected the safety of workers at the farm. The owner of the farm believes that the information that led to the USDA inspectors obtaining the warrants was gathered in a secret inspection of certain portions of the farm. He believes that USDA inspectors broke in at night and then lied on their warrant applications when they stated that they had been tipped off by an informant. Proceedings on the citations are in preliminary stages, and the USDA has acknowledged that if the evidence was illegally obtained, it could not be used against the egg farmer. The owner wants to sue the individual USDA inspectors for damages for violating his constitutional rights. What result? _____

76. Assume the inspectors in the problem above claim that they learned that the egg farmer was about to destroy evidence of serious violations and that there was no time to seek a warrant. Thus, they justify the search based on a belief that they had exigent circumstances allowing a warrantless search. Further, the first federal court opinion on whether exigent circumstances could justify such a search in similar circumstances was not handed down until after the search was conducted. Does this set of circumstances give rise to a defense? _____

77. Assume the same facts as above except, in addition, the administrative law judge rules that the evidence can be used against the egg farm despite the fact that it was seized in violation of the Fourth Amendment. May the administrative law judge be sued under *Bivens* for damages for violating constitutional rights? _____

78. Assume a city building inspector denies a building permit without providing a hearing for the applicant. Further assume that due process requires a hearing before the permit can be finally denied. Is the city liable for the damages caused by this violation?

_____

CHAPTER 13

FREEDOM OF INFORMATION AND OPEN MEETINGS

79. NHTSA pays a private institute to research the driving habits of owners of sport utility vehicles (SUVs). As part of the study, NHTSA instructs the institute to use a control group of drivers of Ford Taurus and Honda Accord automobiles. An insurance industry group pays the same institute to study seat belt usage in all drivers. The institute, to save money, includes both sets of questions in the same study and uses the same drivers (SUV, Taurus, and Accord) for both the driving habits and seat belt usage studies. The institute turns the data regarding SUV drivers over to NHTSA, the data regarding seat belt usage over to the insurance industry group, but keeps the data regarding the driving habits of Taurus and Accord owners in its files because of methodological problems with that part of the survey. The institute informs the agency that it will redo that part of the study. A consumer protection and government watchdog organization would like to see all of the data and argues that because government funds subsidized the control group and the seat belt research, all the data belong, at least in part, to NHTSA. Further, the consumer group claims that the Taurus and Accord data will show that NHTSA chose the institute because of political favors, not because of the quality of the institute's work. Which, if any, of these data are subject to FOIA disclosure? _____

80. Cost overruns are plaguing the design and manufacture of a new Army boot. A competitor of the bookmaker makes a FOIA request for records related to the design and manufacture of the boot. The Secretary of Defense denies the request, claiming that it would reveal secret national defense records. On judicial review, would the Secretary's denial be upheld? _____

81. A drug addiction advocacy group is trying to gather information on how federal agencies treat employees with drug problems. Are personnel records of employees with drug addiction treatment in their files subject to FOIA disclosure? _____

82. A discharged FBI agent seeks judicial review of the agency's decision to fire him. In discovery, he requests files relating to his last ten assignments to show that he performed all assignments competently. He also seeks any communication from the President to the Attorney General and/or to the Director of the FBI. Does the FBI have arguments for withholding this material from discovery? _____

83. A member of the FCC has lunch with a member of the Council of Economic Advisors. At that lunch, they discuss the economics of the marketplace in digital cellular communications and the likely economic effects of various possible regulatory regimes. Did they violate the Sunshine Act? _____

ANSWERS TO
SHORT-ANSWER QUESTIONS

1. **No.** While a great deal of administrative law grows out of the APA, administrative law also has sources in constitutional law (especially separation of powers norms) and in the common law of administrative review that governed before the passage of the APA. The particular statutes governing specific agencies are also important sources of administrative law. With regard to agency procedures, the APA, constitutional due process norms, and particular agency statutes all contribute to the procedural universe.

2. **Administrative agencies distribute benefits, grant permits and licenses, and make and administer policy across a broad range of issues.** As government regulation and government benefits distribution have increased, so have the number of agencies and the range of responsibilities of the agencies.

3. **Public interest theories focus on the policy reasons for agency action,** such as eliminating harmful pollution or redistributing wealth to poor people unable to acquire it in the market or through private charity. **Public choice theories focus on the political activity that leads to agency action** and are more likely to explain regulation and redistribution as the triumph of powerful interest groups who were able to use political clout to secure benefits for themselves from the legislature or agency. For example, while public interest theory would explain the regulation of rates in an industry as necessary to keep prices down while ensuring healthy businesses, public choice theory would explain rate regulation as government protecting businesses from competition that would tend to lower their prices.

4. **No.** Under traditional nondelegation standards, the President's role can be seen largely as "filling up the details." Under the "intelligible principle" test, the requirement that the foreign nation "meets acceptable standards on human rights" is sufficient to pass muster under the nondelegation doctrine.

   The second half of the statute is a bit more problematic because the "best interests of the United States" standard is not very clear. In some contexts this might raise nondelegation concerns. However, a court might view the statute — invoking the universe of considerations that have long been relevant to presidents in trade matters — as supplying an adequate intelligible principle. Further, the President's traditional power in foreign relations makes the relative paucity of guidance more acceptable in this context than in other areas.

5. **Probably not.** The requirements that regulations be submitted to a House committee and that regulations do not go into effect until sixty days after submission are probably constitutional since they do not amount to much of an intrusion into the power of the executive branch and since they become law independent of the action of any unit of Congress. The bicameralism and presentment of the disapproval bill saves it from *Chadha* problems. The constitutionally suspect aspect of the statute is that the vote of the House Ways and Means Committee to disapprove the regulation further postpones the effectiveness of the regulation. Since this action has effects outside the legislative branch of government, it is probably legislative. Thus there would be a violation of *Chadha*'s requirement that any legislative action having legal effect must go through both houses and be presented to the

President. The argument in favor of the constitutionality of this scheme is that the action of the committee merely delays the effective date of the regulation. The regulation is not canceled without passage of a bill by both houses and presentment to the President; this meets *Chadha*'s concerns.

6. **One may be, but not the other.** The good-cause requirement is probably constitutional; the senatorial role in the removal process is not. Despite the predominant understanding of *Myers v. United States,* Congress has broad power to impose good-cause restrictions on the President's ability to fire executive officials. This is made clear from *Morrison v. Olson,* which allowed a good-cause restriction on the firing of an independent counsel. The argument against the good-cause restriction is that by restricting the President's ability to fire a member of the cabinet who reports directly to the President, it infringes on the President's ability to function as a separate, co-equal branch of government and thus violates the separation of powers. On the Senate's role, the cases are clear that Congress, or units of Congress, may not itself participate in the removal process. That provision is unconstitutional.

7. **No.** The comptroller general is removable by a joint resolution of both houses of Congress. Most of the functions of the comptroller general are in aid of the legislative process, and it is thus constitutional for that official to be removable by Congress. However, an official removable by Congress may not exercise authority under the laws of the United States, and this would include the power to disapprove of the Secretary of Transportation's allocation of highway funds.

8. **Probably yes.** The Appointments Clause allows Congress to grant the power to appoint "inferior officers" to the President alone, to the department heads, and to the courts of law. After *Morrison v. Olson* and *Edmond v. United States*, a United States attorney would probably by considered an inferior officer since the United States attorney is subject to the control of the Attorney General and must follow Justice Department policies. As an inferior officer, the United States attorney is subject to appointment by the courts of law. The two arguments against this statute are: a United States attorney is a principal officer and must be appointed by the President with the advice and consent of the President, and the presidential appointment of United States attorneys is necessary to preserve the President's power under a separation of powers analysis. Note that Congress may not grant appointment power for inferior officers to officials not listed in the Appointments Clause and may not itself participate in the appointment of officers of the United States except through Senate confirmation of presidential appointments.

9. **Probably yes.** Because they lack significant discretion and authority to administer the law, the claims officers would probably be considered "employees," not officers of the United States covered by the Appointments Clause. The contrary argument, based on the Supreme Court's decision in *Freytag v. Commissioner of Internal Revenue*, 501 U.S. 848 (1991), in *Landry v. FDIC*, 204 F.3d 1125 (D.C. cir. 2000) would be that processing claims and making recommendations means that they are officers covered by the Appointments Clause and thus must be appointed either by the President with the Advice and Consent of the Senate, or by the Secretary of DHS if Congress so specifies. The D.C. Circuit's decision supports the argument that they are employees.

10. **True.** The problem with the Line Item Veto Act in *Clinton v. NY* was that the President exercised the line item veto after signing the bill. Signing the bill enacts the entire bill into

law. By exercising the line item veto power, the President would be amending or repealing a law that was already in effect, which can only be done through the Constitution's procedure for passing a bill, i.e., bicameralism and presentment. In *Clinton v. NY,* 524 U.S. 417 (1998), the Court stressed that the Constitution preempts the field; Congress cannot alter constitutionally required procedures. The Constitution does not give the President (whether he signs the bill first or not) the right to participate in the legislative process and make decisions regarding the substance of bills except through the veto power.

If, however, the procedures in the Act were included in each appropriations or tax relief bill through incorporation by reference, the constitutional objections may be satisfied. In effect, each bill would provide that the President can elect to cancel certain provisions, and the cancellation power would be part of the law (similar to delegated authority regarding tariffs that the Supreme Court upheld long ago). If the bill itself allows the President to knock out spending and tax benefits, perhaps the President would not be amending or repealing the law by exercising the power but, rather, would be exercising the discretion granted in the bill. If the Act is written into the bill itself, then there is never a problem of the President changing the bill. The only question remaining would be whether a nondelegation doctrine problem exists, and the deficit reduction, without harming the national interest goals of the Act, would provide an intelligible principle.

11. **False.** While Congress can appoint purely legislative officials, any official that exercises significant authority pursuant to the laws of the United States is an "officer of the United States" and must be appointed according to the Appointments Clause of the Constitution. Principal officers must be appointed by the President, and Congress can vest the appointment of inferior officers in the President, courts of law, or heads of departments. Congress may not ever participate in the appointment of an officer of the United States except through the Senate's confirmation power. While at one time it appeared that the Court accepted the view that an official exercising legislative rulemaking power was an agent of Congress and not of the executive branch, today it is clear that any official exercising legal authority must be appointed pursuant to the Appointments Clause.

Congress can restrict the President's removal of an official if, by doing so, it would not interfere with the President's exercise of the executive power and his constitutionally appointed duty to take care that the laws are faithfully executed. After *Morrison v. Olson,* Congress has broader power to restrict presidential removal powers. If the removal restrictions do not violate general separation of powers norms (and do not expressly violate the Constitution), they are permissible. The old rule in *Humphrey's Executor* and *Myers* may have been that Congress may restrict removal only when the official exercises quasi-legislative or quasi-judicial functions and not when the official was purely executive. However, *Morrison* abolished these rigid distinctions. The question is whether the removal restriction impermissibly interfere with the President's authority and duty.

12. This presents an issue of the nondelegation doctrine. While at first glance it may appear that an agency should not be able to establish something as important as the rates of taxation, as long as the intelligible principle standard is met the Constitution should allow this delegation.

The history of delegations indicates that taxing powers have often been delegated. For example, presidential power over tariffs on imported goods has long been held proper, and such tariffs were the most important source of income for the federal government before the Constitution was amended to allow the income tax. The Court would require that Congress make the basic decision about the form of taxation and guide the Secretary's discretion with an intelligible principle. While it may be argued that the nondelegation doctrine should be more strict when it comes to something as important as establishing income tax rates, the Court has not been receptive to arguments that in particular areas the doctrine should be stricter. For example, the Court held that a heightened standard did not apply to the power delegated to the Attorney General to add substances to the list of controlled substances, which in effect created new categories of crimes.

13. **No.** It is important to maintain the distinction between jurisdiction and reviewability. Jurisdiction means that a court may hear a claim, assuming a claim is available. Reviewability is concerned with whether, assuming jurisdiction, a particular agency action can be reviewed. While any claim alleging that an administrator has failed to obey the statute governing her agency may arise under federal law for the purposes of federal question jurisdiction, there are many claims that ultimately cannot be brought because the challenged agency action is unreviewable.

14. **Maybe not.** There are two sets of arguments against review. First, it can be argued that the denial of emergency assistance is not final since the agency will ultimately decide whether the person is entitled to regular or interim benefits. Against this, it can be argued that the denial of emergency benefits amounts to a final determination that the applicant does not meet the criteria for emergency benefits. The second argument is that by providing for judicial review of denials of interim benefits and regular benefits, Congress has implicitly precluded review of denials of emergency benefits. This argument could be strengthened or weakened with evidence from the legislative history and practice regarding other, similar, programs.

15. Now the arguments against reviewability are much stronger. First, interim benefits determinations look even more like tentative decisions regarding the application than do emergency benefits determinations. Because interim-benefits determinations are completely tied to the likelihood that regular benefits will be granted, the decision to deny interim benefits does not seem final. Second, the fact that Congress granted reviewability over one form of temporary relief (emergency) but not another (interim) is strong evidence that Congress did not intend for there to be review of interim determinations. There would be a strong argument that Congress precluded review of interim benefits determinations.

16. **Maybe.** It can be argued that the failure to answer a petition for immediate, emergency action is ripe for review as a refusal after a resonable time has expired, and that a week is too long for a response to a petition for emergency food aid.

17. **Probably not,** on the grounds that the agency action is committed to agency discretion by law. First, the statute does not contain a standard under which the administrator is supposed to decide which sites are given priority treatment. Thus, there may be "no law to apply." Law to apply may, however, be found in the goals of the cleanup program as a whole. Second, the statute explicitly places the priority status determination in the "discretion of the Administrator." This provision may be a "deeming" clause under which judicial review is precluded. Third, it can be argued that this is a decision like prosecutorial discretion because it involves a delicate and expertise-laden balancing of the priorities of the agency. Thus, it is in a category of determinations that are traditionally unreviewable.

18. The court may, under *Norton v. Southern Utah Wilderness Alliance*, dismiss the claim because the claim does not identify "agency action" with sufficient particularity to merit judicial review.

19. Probably yes. Under the legal right test, AT&T would not have had standing because AT&T has no legal right to have its competitors regulated properly. However, under *Data Processors*, AT&T could have standing if it could show that it is injured by the agency action and that it is within the zone of interests in the sense that competitors' interests are relevant to the regulatory scheme governing long-distance telephone service. Since AT&T is in direct competition with MCI and Sprint in the long-distance market, AT&T is probably injured by a loosening of regulatory requirements on its competitors. The more tricky question is whether competitors' interests were relevant when the system of longdistance rate regulation was established. It is likely that such interests were relevant so that AT&T would meet the zone of interests test and have standing to challenge the FCC's treatment of its competitors.

20. Possibly. There are several ways to look at this question. Answering it is difficult because of the lack of consistency in the Supreme Court's standing cases. On the one hand, there are cases that support the argument that standing is lacking because the child's economic difficulties are caused by the noncustodial parent and not by the state. Redressability is also a problem because even if the state tried, it might not be able to establish paternity or procure an enforceable child support order. On the other hand, if you view the child as having a right arising from the state's attempt to establish paternity and to procure the support order, if the state fails to try, you can argue that the injury arises from the state's failure to act. That injury is then sufficient to confer standing in a suit to force the state to try. In general, the Supreme Court has been skeptical of injury in cases like this. Because the purpose of the statute is to force states to try to procure paternity judgments and support orders for persons who are eligible for AFDC benefits, the plaintiff is in a class of the intended beneficiaries of the statute and might have an injury — even if he or she cannot establish that the state would have been successful in the particular case.

21. Maybe. The question is whether the case is ripe for review. Review should normally await an enforcement action, when the illegality of the regulation could be raised as a defense. In *Abbott Labs,* the Supreme Court decided that a regulation can be reviewed pre-enforcement if the issue is "fit" for review, and the regulated party would suffer substantial "hardship" if review was postponed. Here, the issue is probably fit since the only issue is likely to be whether the agency has the legal authority to impose the rule. There is also probably sufficient hardship since printing the labels would be expensive and reveal information that the company would prefer to keep secret. Further, a substantial fine and destruction of stock without proper labels would also be sufficient hardship.

22. The original meaning is that a statute is so vaguely drafted that there is no law to apply to judge whether the agency has violated the statute. In more recent cases the court has also found an action to be committed to agency discretion by law when the action is in a category traditionally not subject to judicial review. This was a reason given in *Lincoln v. Vigil* for not subjecting the allocation of funds from a lump-sum appropriation to judicial review. Finally, the Court has looked at the language of enabling acts to determine whether the statute appears to assign final, unreviewable discretion to the agency without mentioning judicial review. The Court focused on Congress's use of the word "deem" in the statute granting the director of the CIA power to fire employees to support its conclusion that firing CIA employees is committed to agency discretion by law. These statutory provisions can be called "deeming clauses." The last two meanings appear to be newly created since there is no authority or legislative history to support them before *Webster v. Doe.*

23. Without the second part of the question, it is unlikely that the store owner would have standing to challenge the cutoff. First, the store owner would probably not be within the zone of interests, since Congress's concern would be feeding needy people, not supporting stores. (The fact that the food stamp program is administered by the Department of Agriculture and benefits farmers by keeping a strong market for food products undercuts this argument.) Second, although the shopkeeper may be injured by the cutoff if it could be shown that sales went down, the shopkeeper would be asserting the rights of third parties, i.e., the food stamp recipients. Presumably, those people would be able to assert their own rights to the food stamps.

If it were shown that Congress was concerned with food stores when it passed the food stamp program, the zone of interests test might not be a problem. However, the food stamp owners would still be asserting the rights of third parties. The legislative history might make a court more receptive to arguments that the recipients may not assert their own rights, perhaps because finding a lawyer for such small claims might be difficult or because they are very poor and might not understand their rights. The third-party rights issue would not be as serious if the store owner raised a general challenge to the operation of the program as opposed to particular reasons why certain people should continue receiving benefits.

24. **No.** Despite Supreme Court dicta to the contrary, the proper standard of review of rules promulgated pursuant to APA §553 is the arbitrary or capricious standard of APA §706(2). The fact that the department held public hearings does not change this because the substantial evidence test applies only to rules made pursuant to APA §§556-557 and rules made "on the record after hearing" (not to rules made pursuant to §553 even if the agency elects to hold informal public hearing of the sort held in this case). "On the record after hearing" means rules made pursuant to a trial-type procedure, not §553 procedures augmented with public hearings.

25. **Yes.** Some of the standards of review enumerated in APA §706 contain explicit textual limitation on when they apply while others do not. The arbitrary and capricious test contains no such limitation, which means that it applies to all reviewable agency action. However, because the arbitrary and capricious test is the most deferential APA standard of review, the person seeking judicial review will always prefer to have another, less deferential, standard apply — such as the substantial evidence test or de novo review.

26. **No.** The court should review the record that was before the agency at the time the decision was made. APA §706 instructs reviewing courts to look at the "whole record" that was before the agency. It is a principle of administrative law that agency action must stand or fall based on the record that the agency considerred when it made its decision. Even when the decision is made informally, courts should first look at the actual material the agency considered when it made its decision and should receive affidavits regarding the decisionmaking process only when the administrative record does not adequately reveal the basis for the agency's decision.

27. **No.** Under APA §706, the reviewing court is instructed to review the whole record, not merely those parts of it that support the agency. If there was enough evidence (especially documentary evidence), contrary to the agency's doctor's testimony such that a reasonable person would not accept the agency's conclusion, then the agency's decision would not be supported by substantial evidence. This reverses the pre-APA practice under which some courts looked only at the evidence supporting the agency to determine whether the agency's decision was supported by substantial evidence.

28. There are two competing traditions. On one view, the definition of "family unit" is an issue of law for courts to resolve — with some moderate deference to the agency's view. The other tradition is for a highly deferential review, especially if the case involves applying the definition to the particular household. Under *Chevron,* the court would ask whether Congress has directly spoken to the issue. Some members of the Supreme Court would insist that only the plain meaning of the statute should be consulted on this question; others would look more broadly into traditional tools of statutory interpretation such as statutory structure and legislative history. Since there is no definition of "family unit" in the statute, the Court would likely hold that Congress has not directly spoken to the issue, and the inquiry would shift to *Chevron* step two under which the Court would ask whether the agency's definition is a permissible construction of the statute. This is a very deferential standard, and the agency's construction is permissible unless it is substantially irrational.

29. **Possibly.** To argue that they were arbitrary and capricious, the challengers should urge the court to carefully review the record before the agency. It appears that the agency's decision is arbitrary and capricious because the agency did not consider alternatives to complete rescission, and it did not adequately explain its decision. The agency unecessarily gave up the lifesaving benefits of airbags that supported its initial requirement without considering a less-drastic alternative and without explaining why it concluded that the lower-force airbags were not sufficient to solve the problems and preserve safety. Further, the agency did not explain why both rescission of the dual airbags requirement and the on/off switch were necessary and may not have considered the alternative of the on/off switch only.

30. **Maybe.** The legislative process is fine for the owners of most of the parcels in the town since the decision was made to increase the side yard requirement based on general considerations (legislative facts), and it was applied to all property owners across the board. The owners of the twelve parcels that were singled out for special treatment have a good argument that due process requires that they be given notice and a hearing. The relevant facts look like adjudicative facts. Under the *Londoner* case, an adjudicatory hearing may be required as a matter of due process.

31. **Probably yes on both questions.** Although the legislature may have intended that the definition of unfair practices would be developed in the course of adjudications, the statute grants the agency power to make rules. Even though the statute appears to grant the power to make procedural rules and not substantive rules, courts are usually very willing to recognize rulemaking power because of the policy advantages of rulemaking over case-by-case policymaking in adjudications.

32. **No.** There are federal agencies, such as the NLRB, that often announce new rules in the course of adjudication. This practice has been justified on two grounds, against the argument that the APA requires that rules be made in rulemaking. First, it is within

the traditional adjudicatory process for rules to be announced in opinions and then to be applied as binding precedent in subsequent adjudications. Second, in the subsequent adjudications, the rule will be applied only in the context of an order directed against the subject of that particular adjudication. So long as all the procedural rights of the subject of the subsequent adjudication are followed, the order is proper.

33. **No.** If the eight-foot requirement is treated by the agency as binding, it is a new legal requirement — not merely a reminder of what the statute itself always required because the statute does not set forth a height requirement. The agency will argue that the eight-foot requirement merely interprets the meaning of "sufficient structural strength to contain the animals," but this is a weak argument especially because the agency had previously approved shorter fences. In any case, because an interpretative rule is not a binding norm, the agency should have to defend its interpretation on judicial review or in enforcement actions. The agency's interpretation would not bind the courts.

34. **No.** Unless the governing statute indicates otherwise, the Secretary was free to make the decision without a formal procedure because it is not a rule and because the decision does not focus on the conduct or rights of an individual such that adjudication would be required. There is also an argument that §553 would not apply because the decision was about agency organization. There are many situations in which agencies make decisions informally, i.e., without a rulemaking or adjudicatory process. In response to any complaints from Wisconsin, the Secretary is required, by APA §555(e), to provide a statement of the reasons for the decision.

35. **Probably not.** Oil companies will argue that the NPRM did not give adequate notice that reformulation of gasoline, instead of redesign of automobile gas tanks, would be considered. For notice to be adequate, the final rule must be the logical outgrowth of the proposal; the final rule must not be a material alteration of the proposal. The purpose of the notice requirement is to ensure that interested parties know when their interests are at stake, and the oil companies would argue that they had no idea that their product would be the subject of the rulemaking. If the NPRM had mentioned the possibility of other solutions, including reformulation of gasoline, then the oil companies' argument would be weaker. Nevertheless, the oil companies could still argue that absent more specific notice, the EPA should be required to issue a new NPRM focusing specifically on gasoline. However, if the reviewing court applies a more literal reading of §553's notice requirement, it might uphold the notice as adequate because it apprised the public of the subject of the rulemaking — gasoline fumes.

36. **Possibly.** Even though §553 does not address them, ex parte contacts are frowned upon in the rulemaking process. Some courts, on a variety of legal theories, have held that administrators should not willingly receive ex parte contacts; if they do receive them, they should place them on the record for other parties to comment upon. In this case, if the ex parte comments were not part of the record (so that opposing interests had no opportunity to comment upon General Motors' assertion that there would be a negative effect on car makers, and that fact was important to the agency's decision), then there would be a strong argument that the agency should reopen the comment period to allow additional comments on that issue. However, some lower courts have held that ex parte contacts are allowed unless they are statutorily banned, and it violates *Vermont Yankee* to bar them

without a statutory basis. Note that the regulation of ex parte contacts is less strict here than in adjudication, where ex parte contacts are strictly forbidden.

37. **Maybe.** The tobacco companies could argue that the Administrator has an "unalterably closed mind" in his mission against tobacco and that he should thus be disqualified from deciding the rulemaking. Note, however, that there is no mention of prejudgment in informal rulemaking in the APA. *Vermont Yankee* might thus argue against judicial power to disqualify the Administrator on such grounds, unless the tobacco interests could convince the reviewing court that their due process rights were being violated. In addition, this issue raises the conflict between legal norms (which might counsel against allowing someone with such strong views to make a decision like this) and political norms (which favor strong views and a record of accomplishment with regard to those views).

38. **Yes.** The concise general statement should address the major issues raised by the comments. This is an important safeguard against arbitrary decisionmaking. Here, the smokeless tobacco manufacturers raised a significant issue distinguishing their product from other tobacco products, and the Administrator should have explained why he rejected their arguments.

39. **No.** Despite the court of appeals' attempt to link its ruling to the adequacy of the record, the decision violates *Vermont Yankee*, which holds that courts may not impose procedures in addition to those specified by the APA. Here, APA §553 does not provide for cross-examination, and as long as the agency has a rational basis for accepting one side's studies over the other's, the rule should stand.

40. **No.** Formal rulemaking is triggered when the agency is required to make rules "on the record after opportunity for an agency hearing." The statute here does not appear to require that the decision be made "on the record," so even though the statute might create a statutory hybrid, in that an oral hearing must be held, the agency is not required to use formal rulemaking.

41. **Maybe.** This raises a close question under Article III. The Board's jurisdiction is over a private rights dispute, in the core of traditional Article III jurisdiction. On the other hand, the public rights versus private rights divide has been reconceptualized in recent years to be more forgiving of agency jurisdiction over private disputes that are closely related to an area of comprehensive government regulation. NHTSA regulations may be comprehensive, but the branch of the Board's jurisdiction over defective designs is pure products liability law and is traditionally a matter of state law. In favor of the statute's constitutionality is that Article III courts have concurrent jurisdiction—except that a defendant brought before the board has no choice of forum. Also, the board does not have all the attributes of a district court since its orders are not self-enforcing. The deferential standard of judicial review stands against constitutionality. There is no hard and fast answer to whether this statute is constitutional, and there are good arguments on both sides.

42. **No.** The statute does not create an entitlement. Further, procedures do not normally create entitlements, and here the right to procedure is qualified anyway. The only hint of a property interest is the "best interests" standard. However, that standard is vague, and the statute makes it a subjective standard of the sort not generally found to create an entitlement. Barring other promises, or a longstanding practice of termination only for cause, there is no property interest in continued employment.

43. **No.** Section 1 creates an entitlement, i.e., a property interest, to continued employment. A teacher may not be deprived of this interest without due process of law. Section 2 is unconstitutional because, under federal due process law, a hearing is required before the principal may fire a teacher, and the hearing must address whether the standard for cause is met. The amount of process required is determined using the *Mathews v. Eldridge* balancing test, which requires balancing the employee's interest in keeping the job and the accuracy-enhancing value of additional procedure against the government's interest in proceeding without additional procedure. In employment cases, that balance ordinarily requires a hearing in advance of firing. Insofar as section 2 purports to require less than constitutionally adequate procedures, that section is unconstitutional. The argument that claimants should have to take the "bitter" of section 2 with the "sweet" of section 1 was rejected by a majority of the Court in *Arnett v. Kennedy*.

44. **No.** Not all protected interests are determined using entitlement theory. Some such interests are created by the Constitution itself, including the liberty or Fourth Amendment limitations on the use of force in arrests. Thus, Mr. Smith's constitutional rights may have been violated even though state law does not create an entitlement to be free from excessive force.

45. Based on these facts, it is unlikely that a court would find any procedural problem. There is no allegation that the administrative law judge had any personal pecuniary interest in the outcome of the case, and it is unlikely that the fines collected contribute a high percentage of the EPA's budget. If the ALJ's continued employment depended on large fines, then perhaps a bias claim would succeed. There is also no indication that the ALJ is under explicit pressure to rule against violators or impose large fines, although implicit pressure may be problematic. There is also no direct evidence of prejudgment, and unless the ALJ had made a statement regarding the particular case, it is unlikely that a prejudgment claim would be sustained.

46. As long as the FTC has rulemaking authority, and the rule is not ruled arbitrary and capricious on judicial review, the rule may serve to limit the issues at the hearing. Thus, Bad Cereal's objection should be rejected. However, Bad Cereal must be allowed the opportunity to establish that the rule should be waived (for example, by bringing forward evidence that all advertisements and labels show the actual size of the scoops) or that everyone knows that the claim is meaningless. These arguments are likely to fail.

47. **True.** Determining whether due process requires a preexpulsion hearing involves a two-step inquiry. First, there must be an entitlement that creates a life, liberty, or property interest. If such an interest exists, it is then necessary to determine how much process is due.

In evaluating whether a student has a property interest in remaining at a state university, the question is whether any positive law (*Roth*) or assurances and practices (*Perry*) create an entitlement to the state education. It is very likely that students are evaluated on a specific set of criteria, such as a grade point average. Even if the test is more subjective, like "adequate academic performance," there is an entitlement. Due process would be required before a student could finally be expelled. Contrast a situation in which the school can expel students at will — in which case there would be no entitlement. Once an entitlement is established, the next question is how much process is due in order to determine whether the criteria are met. It is very important to separate the substance from the procedure. In other words, generally the criteria set up an entitlement and a hearing is meant. Thus, in the case of a state law requiring good cause to fire an employee, a state teacher who was assaulting students would still be entitled to a hearing. The performance is relevant to the outcome, but even if the teacher would lose, the entitlement still exists.

However, despite the need to separate the entitlement from the process, due process does not always require *full* process like an adjudicatory hearing before action can be taken. Typically, the determination of what process is due requires a balancing of three factors set out in *Mathews v. Eldridge.* Here the private interest is important but not as important as the welfare rights in *Goldberg* or perhaps even the disability benefits in *Mathews.* Accuracy is an important issue. If the criteria for expulsion are clear, like a particular grade point average (GPA), then it can be argued that a hearing before expulsion would add very little in terms of accuracy, since the GPA can be determined from the student's academic paper record. The government may not have a very strong interest in removing students immediately when the issue is academic deficiency, but if the criteria are objective, there is no need for a preexpulsion hearing. If the criteria are more subjective, then the student has a stronger claim that expulsion should not occur without the student being allowed to present his or her own side of the story to try to persuade the decisionmakers that he or she is qualified to remain in school.

48. This raises the general question of whether an adjudicatory decisionmaker must be completely insulated from agency control. The welfare benefits were considered property in *Goldberg* because the terms of the program created an entitlement to the benefits. Because the benefits are property, recipients must be afforded due process before their benefits can be denied or terminated. One basic due process right is the right to a neutral decisionmaker. Here there is no suggestion of prejudgment. The question boils down to whether a decisionmaker must be considered biased if he or she is subject to the type of agency control here — merit pay, removal for cause, and discipline by the agency head. Nothing in the question suggests that the agency has targeted ALJs based on their decisionmaking record, i.e., based on how often they grant or deny benefits. If it were shown that the agency was giving raises for more denials or punishing ALJs for too many grants of benefits, that would present bias due to a pecuniary interest in the outcome of the cases. If the pattern of discipline and pay raises is based on other factors, such as numbers of cases resolved and numbers of reversals in both directions, then there may not be a problem. In general, the Supreme Court has allowed agencies to combine functions as long as there is not specific evidence of bias. Of course, the agency could not violate any of the particular protections of the APA, such as ex parte contacts or direct supervision of the ALJ by the official presenting the agency's case, but the presence of those particular safeguards actually strengthens the argument that the general structure here does not automatically violate due process.

49. No. The agency is not required, by general "reasonableness" language, to regulate only when justified by cost-benefit analysis. Cost-benefit analysis would be required only if the statute clearly required it (for example, by stating that the agency "may impose a requirement only when the benefits achieved by the requirement are greater than the costs of imposing the requirement"). However, under accepted principles, the agency may be required to explain why it chooses to impose the requirement when costs may outweigh benefits and the agency may, if it chooses, reject the requirement on the grounds that it is not cost-effective.

50. **Yes.** These are actual effects on the human environment that must be addressed in an EIS. The disruption of the social structure of the neighborhood is the sort of impact that must be addressed in the EIS.

51. **No.** NEPA does not impose a substantive requirement that agencies minimize the environmental effects of their actions. To comply with NEPA, agencies must prepare an adequate EIS and consider the environmental effects in making their decisions. Here, the agency appears to have considered the environmental effects of its proposal. Even though agency convenience may appear to be a rather weak reason to incur substantial environmental damage, the agency has met its NEPA obligations.

52. **No.** The matter is in the control of the President, not the agency. An agency is not required to address environmental effects of actions over which it has no control.

53. The court should remand the matter to the agency because in general, on judicial review, the agency may defend its decision only on the grounds relied upon in its initial denial.

54. **Yes.** The agency may have an obligation to treat like cases alike. If the current case is different from prior cases, or if the agency has decided to change its policy, it must explain either the differences or the reasons for the change.

55. **No.** Agencies are not estopped by the representations of their officials, especially when the result of estoppel would be to pay money from the treasury in violation of the restrictions placed on such payments by Congress.

56. Not unless there is a clear statutory provision requiring the EPA to act on this type of complaint. Agencies normally have a great deal of discretion in choosing how to use their enforcement resources. If a person petitions the agency and the agency denies the petition, the denial may not be subject to review because courts hold that most enforcement decisions are "committed to agency discretion by law."

57. **Probably not.** Unless the manufacturer can show that the failure to bring enforcement actions against other makers of minivans has no basis, it is no defense to an enforcement action to claim that enforcement should be brought against a competitor as well. The legal standard is "patent abuse of discretion." Because the manufacturer is unlikely to be significantly injured in its ability to compete with other minivan makers, any discriminatory enforcement claim is likely to be very weak. An agency is normally free to proceed one company at a time. The most successful discriminatory enforcement claims are those that raise equal protection concerns, such as a pattern of enforcing regulations against a particular racial group — but even claims like that are difficult to sustain.

58. **Yes.** First, the immediate suspension without a hearing may have violated due process. Occupational licenses are usually property under the *Roth* line of cases, and due process may require a hearing before an agency may suspend a license unless there is evidence of an immediate threat to public health or safety. Further, the composition of the Board presents a problem under *Gibson,* although perhaps not a serious one. If the Board is dominated by lawyers who do not practice under trade names, and they are attempting to destroy competition from another segment of the profession, then there is a problem. They may be biased because of self-interest in the outcome of the hearing. However, it is not clear that the Board is actually in a different market segment from the firms using trade names. This regulation applies to all lawyers, and thus the Board members are limiting

their own activities by enforcing this rule. Further, the big firms may not be in competition with this "legal clinic" and thus the members of the Board may have no personal interest in the outcome. There may be no client of The Legal Clinic who could afford to hire a big-firm lawyer.

59. No. While Murdoch is correct that in normal circumstances the FCC must hold a comparative hearing to award a new license among competing applicants, the FCC may promulgate substantive licensing standards and deny applications that, on their face, fail the standard. Here, if the limit on the number of stations is part of a valid regulation (and there is no dispute that Murdoch owns more than the maximum), the FCC may deny his application without a hearing and award the frequency to the competing applicant. However, if Murdoch's application raises a potentially valid ground for waiving the rule in the particular case, the FCC must provide Murdoch with a hearing on that argument and must explain why it has rejected the argument. Recall that the 1996 Telecommunications Act eliminates the comparative hearing requirement for contested renewals.

60. Yes. The ratemaking process is normally formal adjudication. Here, the Secretary communicated ex parte with an official and received key information from that official without allowing the sellers of natural gas an opportunity to address that information at the hearing. This violates the sellers' procedural rights.

61. False. *Heckler* says that there is a presumption against reviewing agency refusals to take enforcement action against a third party. In claims of discriminatory enforcement, the target of enforcement is arguing for a stay of an order against it until similar orders are issued against others engaging in similar behavior — not for an order requiring the agency to prosecute someone else. The *Moog* case held that, in claims of discriminatory enforcement, an agency's discretionary determination to issue an order against one party, without prosecuting competitors, should not be overturned in the absence of a patent abuse of discretion. While this is a very deferential standard, it is still theoretically possible for an agency order to be delayed.

Heckler does, however, indicate that courts should be reluctant to issue anything that looks like an order for an agency to prosecute. Thus, the argument can be made that after *Heckler,* the enforcement decision is entirely within the agency's discretion, and thus is immune from judicial review. However, in order to find the statement true, one must take a very broad view of *Heckler v. Chaney.* On its face, *Heckler* does not say anything about nonenforcement of an order against a party.

Further, the "never" in the statement is not true even if one takes the broad view of *Heckler,* because the presumption against review is rebuttable. The court stated that the presumption may be rebutted when the substantive statute has provided guidelines for the agency to follow in exercising its enforcement powers. In *Dunlop v. Bachowski,* the court was willing to review an enforcement decision (although the review was *very* deferential) because the statute used clear language and perhaps set out standards for the exercise of the enforcement power. Therefore, even on a broad view, it does not appear that *Heckler v. Chaney* forbids courts from reviewing *any* agency decision related to enforcement, and it should not absolutely bar federal courts from delaying an order based on a valid discriminatory enforcement claim.

62. The first question is whether OSHA has the legal authority to inspect the restaurant, which it probably does as part of its broad workplace safety mission. That mission includes health issues such as the effects of second-hand smoke. The OSHA inspector probably needs a warrant to compel the manager to admit him to the premises since, as to OSHA workplace safety issues, the restaurant is not a pervasively regulated business. However, if OSHA's desire to inspect the restaurant is part of its routine monitoring of workplace safety, then it can probably obtain a warrant without showing that it has reason to believe that the restaurant is violating OSHA standards.

63. **No.** Restaurants would probably be regarded as "pervasively regulated businesses" with regard to Board of Health inspections for proper food-handling practices. The government's interest in regulating restaurant food handling is substantial. Warrantless searches may be necessary to ensure that restaurants don't simply clean up for inspection day. The regulatory scheme's program of regular inspections, and inspections after a complaint, provide the safeguards against arbitrary searches that would otherwise be provided by the warrant procedure. As long as the inspection is part of the normal Board of Health regulatory program, the inspection may take place without a warrant.

64. **Probably yes.** The Court has allowed such requirements in the past. In the particular case, *Wyman v. James,* the Court relied in part on the rehabilitative nature of the home visits, which involved childcare issues. Here, the only purpose is to monitor eligibility, which puts the inspector in a purely adversarial relationship with the recipient. Nevertheless, if the only consequence of not allowing the inspection would be a benefits cutoff, the Court would likely uphold the requirement.

65. **Probably not.** The Court has upheld drug-testing programs when there was a special need for the tests, but it struck down a requirement that candidates for statewide office undergo drug testing. For many government positions not involving law enforcement and where drug abuse would not endanger the public or other employees, the Court would likely hold that the need to be certain about drug abuse was not strong enough to outweigh the prospective employees' privacy interests.

66. **No.** The bank, as a corporation or collective entity of some sort, has no right against self-incrimination. The Fifth Amendment right against self-incrimination protects only natural persons. The bank president, as custodian of corporate records, may not assert his own Fifth Amendment rights even though the act of producing the records amounts to testimony that the records exist, which directly incriminates him of perjury.

67. **No.** The provision allowing injunctions against violators applies to the government only when the government itself is polluting, not when the government allegedly is not regulating properly. Unless the statute requires EPA to ban indoor smoking at workplaces, the Administrator does not fail to fulfill a nondiscretionary duty by not banning smoking in indoor workplaces. Only judicial review may be used to attack the substance of regulations.

68. **Probably.** If a member of the American Lung Association is injured by the failure to ban smoking, e.g., if a member works in an indoor workplace where smoking is allowed, then the Association has standing to assert its member's claim. There should be no zone of interests problem as long as the Association's member is a worker, since it is likely that workers are within the zone of interests of the statute. Further, even if there were a theoretical zone of interests problem, the typical citizens' suit provision places everyone identified as having a claim within the zone of interests.

69. **Maybe.** The Supreme Court has approved a private right of action under statutes like the one described, largely because the plaintiff is clearly within the class of people who benefit from the statute, and the private action would tend to advance the purposes of the statute. However, in the absence of evidence of congressional intent to allow the private right of action, the courts today would be skeptical of the claim. The Supreme Court now appears to agree with Justice Powell's dissent in *Cannon* that judicial creation of a right of action out of a regulatory statute raises serious separation of powers concerns on the ground that it is for Congress to decide whether to create a federal cause of action.

70. **Probably yes.** The federal statute probably regulates the safe use of pesticides and fertilizers because of safety and general environmental concerns. Such statutes often have savings clauses and rarely preempt state tort law. The federal statutes that regulate the labeling of pesticides have been held not to preempt state claims based on improper use of pesticides. However, if the federal statute explicitly preempts claims based on the use of pesticides and fertilizers or if the overall context indicates that Congress intended to preempt such claims, then the state claim might not survive.

71. **No.** A claim that an employer has fired an employee for engaging in pro-union activities states a claim that the employer has committed an unfair labor practice. Such claims are within the primary jurisdiction of the NLRB; it is up to the Board to determine whether the company has committed an unfair labor practice.

72. **No, for several reasons.** First, under the *Feres* doctrine, members of the military may not sue over decisions of their superior officers even if the FTCA might otherwise provide for liability. Second, because the decision involved discretion and choice, the FTCA's discretionary-functions exception bars liability. Third, under state law, it may not be tortious to provide an employee with an automobile without an airbag. Thus, even if the other obstacles to FTCA liability could be overcome, the predicate for FTCA liability (liability for similar conduct under local law) would not be met.

73. **Possibly.** The Supreme Court has rejected an exception to the FTCA for all regulatory functions, so even though the government is playing a purely regulatory role, the FTCA might still be available. If NHTSA approved the car in violation of clear statutory directives, then the discretionary-function exception would probably not bar liability. The *Berkovitz* Court held that there is no discretion to violate mandatory provisions of governing law. However, the plaintiff must establish that the approval of the automobile did not involve choice or policy judgment — that there was no discretion regarding observance of the statutory requirement.

74. **No liability.** Federal officials have immunity from damages for common-law claims based on conduct within the outer bounds of their official duties. It is within the outer bounds of the duties of FTC commissioners to speak on matters of public interest involving advertising, which is within FTC jurisdiction.

75. He probably has a viable *Bivens* claim against the inspectors. Under *Bivens,* victims of Fourth Amendment and other constitutional violations can sue the perpetrators for damages. Even though the exclusionary rule might prevent the use of the evidence in the agency proceedings, it is not a substitute for a damages remedy against the offending officials. Congress has not declared that the USDA procedures are a substitute for the *Bivens* action, and the fact that the USDA applies the exclusionary rule in its proceedings

is not enough to make the existence of those proceedings a "special factor counseling hesitation." While a comprehensive remedial scheme might be a special factor, here the USDA scheme does not really provide a remedy for the Fourth Amendment violation, so it should not displace the *Bivens* action.

76. **Yes.** They may have a qualified immunity defense. Under qualified immunity, officials are not liable unless they violate clearly established constitutional rights of which a reasonable official should know. If the inspectors establish that no similar case had found a Fourth Amendment violation, they would be immune from a damages award. Note that it is not enough that the general right to be free from an unreasonable search and seizure is clearly established. The cases require that it be clearly established that the particular facts alleged establish a constitutional violation.

77. **No.** The ALJ has absolute immunity from damages for constitutional violations in performance of her judicial duties. At common law, judges, legislators, and prosecutors had absolute immunity from damages. Under the functional approach, administrative officials are accorded the same immunities as their nonadministrative counterparts. ALJs thus receive judicial immunity, agency prosecuting officials receive prosecutorial immunity, and agency officials making rules receive legislative immunity.

78. **Maybe.** Municipal liability in this situation depends on many factors. While cities are proper defendants in §1983 cases, they cannot be held liable on a vicarious liability theory. Rather, cities may be held liable only for violations attributable to municipal policy. If the city had an official policy requiring hearings before denials of building permits, then the city cannot be held liable. However, if city policy stated that no hearing was required, or if the building inspector had the final authority under city law to determine whether a hearing would be held, then it would be appropriate to hold the city liable for damages.

79. NHTSA is an agency, and any data turned over to it would be considered part of agency records since they would be obtained by the agency for agency purposes. Thus, the data regarding SUV driving habits would be subject to FOIA disclosure unless further information would reveal that some exemption should apply. The remaining data are likely not to be subject to FOIA disclosure because the data are not in government files. Even if NHTSA has a right to obtain the data, courts have held that FOIA does not obligate agencies to obtain files to make them subject to public disclosure. Thus, even though an important FOIA-related purpose would be served by publication of the flawed Taurus and Accord data, because those data are not part of agency records, they are not subject to FOIA disclosure.

80. **No, unless the records were properly classified.** Records may be withheld as secret national defense records only if the records have been classified as secret pursuant to executive orders creating and regulating the classification system. *See* 5 U.S.C. §552(b)(1). Thus, unless the boot records were properly classified as secret defense records pursuant to an executive order, the Secretary may not withhold them as secret defense records under FOIA.

81. **Maybe.** Exemption (6) exempts from disclosure "personnel and medical files and similar files the disclosure of which would constitute a clearly unwarranted invasion of personal privacy." The test for whether an invasion of privacy is "unwarranted" is a balancing test with the interests in monitoring government activity on one side and the individual's

privacy interests on the other. Raw data, without names and other identifying factors attached, would pose very little risk of invasion of privacy and thus might be available under FOIA. Any information, however, which might lead to identification of drug-addicted federal employees would not be subject to FOIA disclosure.

82. **Yes.** The FBI may have an evidentiary privilege if it can show a judge that release of the material would damage important law enforcement interests. Further, the FBI might assert executive immunity to resist revealing the contents of any communication from the President to the Director of the FBI. On the claim of executive immunity or privilege, once the claim is made, the party seeking the material has the burden of establishing that the material is vital to achieving justice in the proceeding. The plaintiff's interest in obtaining the material is substantial but is not as weighty as the interest of a criminal defendant's in obtaining material important to defending a criminal prosecution.

83. **No, because the lunch was not a meeting of an agency.** A meeting constitutes a meeting of an agency only when there is a possibility that agency business will be conducted. There is no suggestion that a single FCC commissioner or a single member of the Council of Economic Advisors has the power to conduct agency business alone.

ESSAY EXAM
QUESTIONS
AND
ANSWERS

ESSAY EXAM
QUESTIONS AND ANSWERS

The following questions were asked on various Boston University Law School Administrative Law examinations. The questions are reproduced as they actually appeared, with only slight modifications. The sample answers are not "official" and represent merely one approach to handling the questions.

QUESTION 1: (Note: This is a fictionalized version of an actual case. Parts A and B are not necessarily of equal weight.)

Section 404 of the Clean Water Act (the Act) authorizes the United States Army Corps of Engineers (the Corps) to issue permits "for the discharge of dredged or fill material into the navigable waters." Section 301(a) of the Act provides that the "discharge of any pollutant by any person" is unlawful unless in compliance with the Act's permit requirements. Discharge, in turn, is defined as "any addition of any pollutant to navigable waters from any point source." *Id.*

The statute was prompted because often the least expensive way to dispose of dredged material is to redeposit it at another place in the navigable water. This can disrupt the ecology of the waterway, and may also cause serious pollution if the dredged material contains harmful pollutants. This happens often, for example, when harbor areas or areas suffering from previous industrial discharges are dredged.

In 1977 the Corps promulgated regulations that generally tracked the statutory language, defining "discharge of dredged material" as "any addition of dredged material into the waters of the United States," with a few limited exceptions. 42 Fed. Reg. 37,145 (July 19, 1977). A new regulation, issued in 1986, exempted from the permit requirement "de minimis, incidental soil movement occurring during normal dredging operations." 51 Fed. Reg. 41,232. Although this regulation did not define "normal dredging operations," its preamble gave some guidance as to the exemption's coverage:

> Preamble: Section 404 clearly directs the Corps to regulate the discharge of dredged material, not the dredging itself. Dredging operations cannot be performed without some fallback. However, if we were to define this fallback as a "discharge of dredged material," we would, in effect, be adding the regulation of dredging to section 404 which we do not believe was the intent of Congress. *Id.* at 41,210.

After the regulation was issued, there was some controversy over its coverage. All agree that the 1986 rule did regulate "sidecasting," which involves placing removed soil in the same waterway but at some distance from the point of removal. *See* 58 Fed. Reg. 45,008, 45,013 (Aug. 25, 1993) (noting that sidecasting has "always been regulated under Section 404"). However, there was disagreement over whether the regulation covered "redeposit" and "fallback." Redeposit occurs when material removed from the water is returned to it at the same general location. When redeposit takes place at substantially the same time as the initial removal, for example, when material falls back in while dredging is being done, it is referred to as "fallback." A regulation was promulgated, and it required that once material was removed, a permit should be required to redeposit the material or to allow the material to fall back. In response to an argument that was raised in comments received after the regulation was promulgated, the Corps issued (without notice and comment) an interpretative rule providing that "the permit requirements do not apply to redeposit and fallback." The agency stated, in a statement accompanying the interpretative rule, that redeposit of material dredged from the waterway poses little (if any) threat to the cleanliness or navigability of the waterway.

Part A. In 1992, a developer sought to dredge 700 acres of wetlands in North Carolina. *See* 58 Fed. Reg. at 45,016. Because the developer's efforts involved only minimal incidental releases of soil and other dredged material into the neighboring waterway, the Corps's field office personnel determined that, under the terms of the 1986 regulation, §404's permit requirements did not apply. In response to the developer's query, the field office director issued a statement to that effect. Environmental groups, concerned by what they viewed as the adverse effects of the developer's activities on the wetlands and the neighboring waterway, filed an action seeking enforcement of the §404 permit requirement. *See North Carolina Wildlife Federation v. Tulloch,* Civ. No. C90-713-CIV-5-BO (E.D.N.C. 1992). The environmental groups made the following claims against the Corps's action:

1. The Corps had not included a discussion, in its EIS required under NEPA, of the effects of "redeposit" and "fallback" on the waterway. The EIS stated merely that redeposit and fallback would have no adverse effects since the material was identical to the material already in the waterway and since only a minimal amount of material would be involved. The environmental groups argued that there was no proof that the material would not be dangerous and that the baseline should be the waterway without the material.
2. The de minimis exception to the permit requirement was arbitrary, capricious, and contrary to the statutory language and thus should be declared void.
3. The interpretative rule is void because it should have been promulgated in a notice and comment procedure.

The environmental groups sought an order requiring the Corps to subject the developer to the permit process. The environmental groups also sued the developer in federal court seeking an injunction against the draining and clearing project, claiming violations of the Clean Water Act, NEPA, and state law.

Please identify and analyze potential defenses the Corps and the developer might have to these claims. Please state explicitly any assumptions you need to make if the facts do not provide sufficient information.

Part B. Assume the portions of the above case against the Corps were settled. As part of the settlement of the case (a settlement to which the developer was not a party), the Corps agreed to propose stiffer rules governing the permit requirements for landclearing and excavation activities. The result (the regulation at issue here) has come to be called the *"Tulloch* Rule." The new rule (rescinding the old regulations) was promulgated after notice and comment, consistent with the settlement agreement. It removed the de minimis exception and expanded the definition of discharge to cover "any addition of dredged material into, including any redeposit of dredged material within, the waters of the United States." 33 CFR §323.2(d)(1). Specifically, the rule defines "discharge of dredged material" to include "[a]ny addition, including any re-deposit, of dredged material, including excavated material, into waters of the United States which is incidental to any activity, including mechanized landclearing, ditching, channelization, or other excavation." 33 CFR §323.2(d)(1)(iii) (emphasis added). The concise general statement provides, inter alia, that the new regulation will minimize the potentially harmful effects of redeposit. The agency also, without notice and comment, rescinded the interpretative rule.

The developer and a trade association (of which the developer is a member) seek immediate judicial review of the rescissions of the former regulation and the interpretative rule and of the issuance of the new regulation. They claim that the Corps lacks power to require a permit for redeposit and fallback under the statutory definition of "discharge."

As part of their investigation, the lawyers for these parties discover that, during the comment period, a manufacturer of dredging equipment demonstrated to Corps officials that new equipment would virtually eliminate fallback. They suspect that this manufacturer has connections to Corps officials and is hoping that the new rule will increase sales of the new equipment because developers will need to eliminate fallback to avoid the permit process. It also appears that the Corps had information that eliminating redeposit, including fallback, would increase jobs in companies specializing in dredging material disposal. Neither the equipment nor the jobs issue was mentioned in the concise general statement.

Please identify and analyze the claims for judicial review and any expected responses from the agency and the environmental groups.

SAMPLE ANSWER TO QUESTION 1

Part A.   First, the defendants — the Corps and the developer (*D*) — can argue that the environmental group lacks standing to file suit. There are three constitutional requirements for standing: 1) injury, 2) causation, and 3) redressability. There are prudential limitations, including the zone of interests requirement. Because the Clean Water Act allows for citizens' suits and theoretically puts all citizens within the zone of interests, the zone of interests test should not be a problem for anyone who otherwise has standing. The Act allows citizens to sue for violation of the substantive provisions of the Act and for the Administrator's failure to perform a nondiscretionary duty. The Act would also allow the group to sue the developer if he's violating the Act by discharging pollutants without a permit. However, the plaintiff environmental group (*P*) still has to meet the constitutional requirements of injury, causation, and redressability.

To prove injury, *P* will have to show that it is harmed by the redepositing or fallback by showing that it uses the waters at issue and that this use is harmed. Assuming some members use the water, the aesthetic injury of observing dirtier water is probably enough for standing and also any appreciable effect on the cleanliness of the water should be enough. The environmental groups will also have to show that the Corps' regulation that exempts incidental soil movement is causing the injury and that subjecting the developer to the permit process will remedy the injury. This means that the regulation must result in more bad stuff ending up in the water.

The standing cases are wildly inconsistent, so it is difficult to predict how a court would come out on this one. Presumably, the plaintiff read *Sierra Club* and *Lujan* and knows to find some member who uses the waters. Whether a court will find that the injury is fairly traceable to the Corps's failure to subject the developer to the permit process is speculative. Presumably if *P* receives an injunction against the developer, that will at least temporarily stop its project. In *SCRAP,* the court found a causal connection between an increase in freight rates and a decrease in recycling, resulting in more litter. But in *EKWRO,* the court didn't find causation in the IRS's grant of charitable status to nonprofits who don't provide emergency medical services to poor people and plaintiffs who were denied the opportunity to receive services there. The trickiest part is whether "harm" to *P* will be stopped by the permit process. If the Corps doesn't think it has authority to regulate fallback, it seems it will likely issue a permit, if required to, to anyone who will only be discharging fallback. The result will be the same — *P* is only trying to add a procedural step. However, some cases would allow standing just based on the chance that the Corps might deny the permit.

Second, assuming standing exists, *D* can try to argue that the suit is not ripe for judicial review. But this is likely to fail. The developer has now acted under the regulations, and the Corps made a final determination that the permit requirements didn't apply in his case. Therefore, in effect, the Corps has enforced the regulation, thus making it final agency action.

Third, the Corps can argue its EIS under NEPA is sufficient. Under *Calvert Cliffs,* an agency must consider the environmental effects as part of its decision in order for the decision not to be arbitrary and capricious. *P* argues the Corps didn't consider the environmental effects of redeposit and fallback and that the EIS merely stated that there would be no adverse effects without any evidence that the matter was considered. The Corps can argue that its statement that the redeposit or fallback of material dredged would not have an adverse effect (since the material was identical to the material already in the waterway) shows that it did consider the effects. It considered it and made a statement about it. Under *Strycker's Bay, P* can't challenge an agency's decision just because the agency may have undervalued the environmental effects. *P* claims there is no proof that the material won't be dangerous, but *P* has not offered proof that the material will be dangerous. Under *Strycker's Bay,* it seems the Corps has to only meet a minimum threshold to satisfy the requirements of the EIS.

Next, *P* argues the de minimis exception is arbitrary, capricious, and contrary to the statutory language. When promulgating the 1986 regulation, the Corps exempted incidental soil movement during normal dredging operations, and in the preamble the Corps said it didn't have the power to regulate dredging and, therefore, couldn't regulate fallback material. This raises the question of whether §404 authorized the Corps to regulate dredging operations, and it raises the question of whether fallback should be defined as discharge of dredged material. Both questions involve statutory interpretation, which should be analyzed under the *Chevron* test. Step one of *Chevron* asks whether Congress has directly spoken to the precise question at issue. If so, Congress's intent prevails. If the agency's interpretation is contrary, the court on review should overrule the agency. There are two interpretations of *Chevron* step one. The original *Chevron* looks only at the plain meaning to determine whether Congress has directly spoken to this precise issue. In this case, Congress did define discharge to include *any addition* of *any* pollutant to navigable waters. The Corps can argue that the *addition* of *any* pollutant does not include fallback or redeposit of material that was already there. But *P* may argue that once the material is out of the waterway during dredging, putting it back or allowing it to fall back clearly meets the statutory definition and thus not only is within the Corps's power to regulate, but the Corps must regulate. Additionally, sidecasting has always been regulated and that is not necessarily adding pollutants in the way the Corps interprets it. The agency will argue that to meet the "directly spoken" standard, Congress would have had to be much more specific about fallback and redeposit. But it is not clear whether Congress has directly spoken about whether the Corps has the power to regulate dredging operations.

The court may apply the *Cardoza-Fonseca* version of *Chevron* step one, which uses traditional tools of statutory interpretation, like legislative history, language, and structure, to decide if Congress addressed the specific issue. Under this analysis, the court is more likely to find Congress did address the issue than under the original *Chevron* analysis. It seems as though the court may find that Congress did address the issue and would agree with the agency's interpretation that discharge does not include fallback or redeposit. It seems unlikely that Congress intended the Corps to regulate the dredging process with its pollution-based permit system.

If the court does not find Congress addressed the issue, it will move to step two, which asks whether the agency's interpretation is permissible and within the range of what Congress contemplated. This is very deferential, and a court will likely side with the Corps and determine that the de minimis exemption is not contrary to the statutory language. Even if the court approves the interpretation, it may ask whether the decision here — to not require a permit — is arbitrary and capricious. The arbitrary and capricious test looks at whether the agency considered all the relevant factors, evaluated alternatives, and explained its conclusions on issues raised in the decisionmaking process. In this case, the Corps determined that dredging operations can't be performed without some fallback, and it determined it didn't have the authority to regulate dredging operations. The arbitrary and capricious test is very deferential. There does not appear to be "clear error" here as defined in *Overton Park*. Its conclusion does not seem to be so implausible that it couldn't be ascribed to a difference in view or product of agency expertise, as discussed in *The Airbags Case*. Therefore, the de minimis exception is likely to be held valid.

Finally, *P* argues the interpretative rule is void because it should have been promulgated through notice and comment. APA §553 exempts interpretative rules from its notice and comment provisions. An interpretative rule is one that clarifies a statutory term or reminds parties of existing duties. However, a legislative rule (which is subject to notice and comment) attempts to supplement the statute, adds to the duties or the law, or changes the law. *P* argues the rule is legislative. In support of its argument, it may argue that the interpretative rule is trying to change the 1986 regulation, and agencies can't change legislative rules with interpretative rules. But the Corps can argue that it is not attempting to change the 1986 regulation or add any duties. Instead, it is merely clarifying what it means by incidental soil movement. The interpretative rule merely explains that incidental soil movement includes redeposit and fallback. The 1986 regulation is an existing statutory norm, and the interpretative rule just explains it further. It is unlike *National Family Planning* (which changed the statutory norm), and it's unlike *Hoctor* (which added the duty to build an eight-foot fence). Here, the Corps restated or clarified what it already said in the 1986 regulation.

Part B. Before the developer and trade association can get judicial review of any claims, they will have to show they have standing. Standing should be fairly easy for the developer. Under the old regulation, he did not need a permit for his dredging operations, but under the new regulation he will need a permit. The permit process itself is probably somewhat costly and time-consuming, which is an injury in itself. And he will likely be injured if he is refused a permit. The trade association is a little more removed, but it should have standing if it meets the normal requirements for associational standing. Because the developer is a member of the association, the association might be able to get standing through him. Additionally, it may have other members directly affected — like the developer.

Next, both will have to show that the suit is ripe for judicial review. In this case, the agency issued a regulation and apparently has not yet enforced it against the developer. Should the developer have to wait for a denial of a permit before seeking review? The first question is whether the agency's act is final. APA §704 provides for judicial review, except where precluded, for final agency action for which there is no adequate remedy in court. The court in *Abbott Labs* said the promulgation of a regulation is final agency action because the process is over. The second question to determine ripeness is whether the issues are fit and whether the party seeking review would suffer hardship if review were delayed until after enforcement. An issue is fit if it is purely legal and does not require additional fact or policy findings. An issue is not fit if it is unclear what its meaning is or when it is likely to be applied. In this case, the issue of whether a permit is required is purely legal and does not require additional findings. Presumably, the regulation applies right away. If the developer wants to begin dredging, he will have to file for a permit. A party will suffer hardship if the regulation is expensive to comply with and if there are substantial impediments to challenging it in an enforcement action. If there is a delay in review, the developer can either apply for a permit (which presumably costs some money) or can go ahead with dredging and risk an enforcement action. The regulation does require a change in the developer's conduct, since he must not dredge until he gets the permit. Depending on the cost of the permit and the delay involved, this may not rise to the same level of hardship as those in *Abbott Labs*. But it is not as little a hardship as in *Toilet Goods*. A court may not find sufficient hardship to determine that the suit is ripe since there is probably not too much money at stake to comply.

Assuming, however, that the suit is ripe, *P* can claim that rescission of the old regulation is arbitrary and capricious and that the issuance of the new regulation in its place is arbitrary and capricious. In *The Airbags Case,* the court reviewed the agency's decision to rescind a regulation under the arbitrary and capricious test. It held that the decision to rescind was arbitrary primarily because the agency didn't consider relevant factors (like the inertia factor), failed to analyze alternatives (like airbags), and failed to explain why it decided the way it did. In this case, there is little information about why the Corps decided the way it did, except that it submitted to pressure from the environmental group that sued it in Part A. There is no new evidence on the record about the harmful effects of redeposit. The general statement just concludes that the regulation will minimize the potentially harmful effects of redeposit. There is absolutely no new evidence to suggest why the Corps switched to this statement after previously concluding that redeposit did not threaten the navigability or cleanliness of the water. And the agency's decision stands or falls based on the rationalizations it made when it promulgated the rule — so it cannot come up with anything new. There are no facts to substantiate the decision to rescind. Therefore, a court should find it arbitrary and capricious. If a court found the decision to rescind was valid, however, then it probably will find this new regulation substantively valid. The arbitrary and capricious standard is deferential and there is nothing wrong per se with a tougher standard, as long as the agency considers all the relevant factors and alternatives. The only problem is that it does not explain how it determined that redeposit is potentially harmful. In other words, it does not explain its conclusions about issues raised in the decisionmaking process. It looks particularly arbitrary because the agency itself may actually agree with the developer but feel legally pressured not to act on its own views. Although we do not know what information it had in the record to substantiate this claim, this might be grounds for finding the regulation arbitrary and capricious.

P can argue there is a problem with rescinding the interpretative rule without notice and comment. Assuming that the interpretative rule is, in fact, an interpretative rule (see discussion Part A), then the agency can change one interpretative rule with another one. The agency could presumably rescind it without notice and comment. *P* might be able to argue that the regulation is void because the agency relied on ex parte information without giving interested parties a chance to comment. Apparently, the Corps had information that eliminating redeposit would increase jobs and that new equipment would virtually eliminate fallback. The agency cannot conceal information that it relied on in making its decision. Interested parties must be afforded a meaningful opportunity to submit comments. In order for the opportunity to be meaningful, parties must have notice of information upon which the agency relies. Also, in the concise general statement, the agency must state the major issues of the policy that were made public in the proceeding, and it must give policy reasons for its decision to choose one course or another. Since the agency did not mention the new equipment or the information about job increases, the court might order a new comment period, when interested parties could reply to this information. It is, however, unclear whether the APA really imposes these obligations.

P can also argue that the agency administrator either prejudged the issue or is biased. The problem is that the standard for showing prejudgment is much tougher for rulemaking than for adjudication. For rulemaking, the standard is clear and convincing evidence that the administrator has an unalterably closed mind on matters critical to the disposition of the proceeding. Proving an unalterably closed mind involves showing, from public or private statements, that the decisionmaker is convinced that the proposed rule is necessary without regard to the substance of the comments received. Apparently, the Corps had ex parte comments with these equipment manufacturers, but it is not apparent that an ex parte contact (in itself) is wrong. *HBO* says, "just say no." *Costle* is not really concerned as long as important contacts be put on the record. Granted, the officials did not put the information on the record, but they could argue it was not important to the decision or the court could order a new comment period. These contacts probably are not sufficient to disqualify the administrator from participating in the proceedings. In fact, based on *Vermont Yankee* (or at least the spirit of *Vermont Yankee*), it is not clear if *Costle* or *HBO* are even valid since the APA does not ban ex parte contacts in rulemaking.

The best evidence of prejudgment is that the Corps settled the case with the environmental group and may have decided to promulgate a stiffer rule regardless of the comments it received. Under the settlement agreement, it said it would propose stiffer rules. This might show an unalterably closed mind — one convinced that a stiffer rule was necessary, regardless of the comments received. However, the key word is "propose." Just as in negotiated rulemaking, the agency was free to adopt a different rule.

Finally, *P* can argue, as the Corps did in Part A, that the agency doesn't have power to regulate dredging operations and interpreting discharge to include redeposit means the Corps will be regulating dredging operations. This may involve using the *Chevron* test again, concerning the meaning of discharge. This time the agency argues it includes redeposit. Assuming Congress didn't address the issue (but see the discussion in Part A), then the agency's interpretation is probably within a permissible range.

QUESTION 2: (Note: The statutes discussed may have been modified for this problem.)

The federal Food, Drug and Cosmetic Act (the Act) prohibits the use of any "drug" as a food additive without the specific approval of the FDA. The Act contains no definition of a "drug."

The FDA is an agency within the Department of Health and Human Services, which is headed by a single commissioner. The Commissioner has the full power to act on behalf of the agency, including issuing policy statements, regulations (and other such things), and the power to review adjudications conducted under the Act. The Act grants the FDA the power to issue "such rules and regulations necessary to carry out the provisions of the Act." The Act also authorizes the FDA to hold hearings on alleged violations and issue fines and cease and desist orders against violations. The Act provides that the initial hearing is held before an administrative law judge "not under the supervision, direct or indirect, of any employee of the Food and Drug Administration." Appeal is to the Commissioner, who has all the power of the initial decisionmaker, with substantial evidence judicial review "in the court of appeals for the circuit in which the party charged has its main place of business or in which the violation is alleged to have taken place, at the option of the parry charged."

Since the passage of the Act, the FDA has interpreted the Act not to cover chemicals found naturally in any food product. Thus it has not regulated the use of caffeine in soft drinks, since caffeine occurs naturally in coffee and chocolate. A 1965 policy statement (issued by its then-commissioner) stated that "[i]t is the policy of the FDA not to require approval for any food additive found naturally in a commonly consumed food product as long as the concentrations of such additive are no greater than concentrations naturally occurring in other food products."

The debate over whether cigarettes should be regulated because of evidence that cigarette manufacturers were carefully setting the amount of nicotine in cigarettes sparked interest in whether soft drink manufacturers were engaged in similar manipulation of the amount of caffeine in soft drinks. Critics cited the advertising of Jolt Cola that "all the sugar and twice the caffeine" was evidence that soft drinks were being spiked with caffeine to maintain sales of soft drinks. Critics also cited evidence that some drinks, such as Mountain Dew and Mellow Yellow, contained as much caffeine per serving as coffee.

In early 1996, the FDA issued a statement providing: "The FDA will now apply the Food, Drug and Cosmetic Act to require approval as additives for all drugs used as food additives, including those that are found naturally in a commonly consumed food product, even if the concentrations of such additives are no greater than concentrations naturally occurring in other food products. Because this is not a legislative rule, section 553 procedural requirements do not apply." The FDA then conducted research on caffeine in soft drinks. Immediately after the issuance of the 1996 FDA statement, several soft drink manufacturers removed caffeine from their products.

Needless to say, soft drink manufacturers and the manufacturers of caffeine additive powder were not happy with this turn of events. They are seeking advice on what steps they might be able to take now to prevent the FDA from going forward with its research. They also wonder whether any other of the FDA's actions thus far violate the APA and can be challenged at this time. You have been hired by the soft drink manufacturers and the caffeine additive manufacturers to provide legal advice on what steps they might take at this point. Early in your research, you discover from a disgruntled FDA employee that before the 1996 statement was issued, the Commissioner of the FDA had extensive contacts regarding the effects of caffeine with health care advocates and, at a private research session, he was shown a great deal of evidence regarding the negative effects of caffeine and the prevalence of caffeine addiction among children who drink Mountain Dew and eat chocolate. Also, the FDA Commissioner generally refused to meet with soft drink and caffeine industry lobbyists, citing potential conflicts of interest.

Part A. Please write a memorandum regarding potential challenges at this stage and any issues that might be available on judicial review at a later stage.

(New facts below for Part B)

Assume that the FDA's research continued and ultimately the FDA enforcement bureau brought an enforcement complaint against Jake Cola, Inc., a small Los Angeles-based manufacturer of high-priced organic cola drinks. Jake Cola contains far less caffeine than the leading brands of cola drinks such as Coca-Cola and Pepsi-Cola. Jake Cola's market share is minuscule; it has approximately less than .1 percent of the market share in the Los Angeles area and only fifty thousand dollars worth of business outside of California, annually. (Assume that this is sufficient to meet any "interstate commerce" requirements for federal regulation.) In fact, Jake Cola advertises that it has less caffeine than the other brands and shows on its label the actual number of milligrams of caffeine per serving, which no other brand does.

In an informal conversation, Jake's lawyer asked the FDA prosecutor why Jake Cola was being singled out at this time. The FDA prosecutor responded that the FDA has an informal policy of prosecuting companies that advertise regarding the additive at issue, and also the FDA usually goes after small companies first to establish a principle that can be applied in later cases against larger companies that, in the words of the prosecutor, "might put up more of a defense." Jake Cola's lawyer then asked whether an enforcement action was being brought against Jolt, which advertises "twice the caffeine." The FDA prosecutor said, "no," and also said he thinks it is related to the fact that Jolt has a lobbyist that used to be general counsel at the FDA.

Part B. Jake Cola's lawyer heard from Jake's caffeine supplier about your earlier work regarding this matter and would like to know whether any of this additional information might either help Jake Cola prevent the hearing from occurring or supply grounds for reversing any adverse decision later on judicial review. Do not address any potential First Amendment issues.

(New facts below for Part C)

Assume that the hearing against Jake Cola went forward. The ALJ, although finding a violation of the Act since Jake Cola admittedly adds caffeine without FDA approval, declined to issue a cease and desist order or impose a fine on the grounds that "Jake Cola is a small player in the soft drink market and uses less caffeine than most. An order should not issue unless other, larger soft drink manufacturers are also prosecuted." The FDA prosecutor then sought review before the Commissioner. The Commissioner, after a full evidentiary hearing, found that Jake Cola was in violation of the Act, that a cease and desist order should issue, and that a fine was not proper at this time. The Commissioner, in the conclusion of his opinion stated the following:

> I hereby find that caffeine is a drug and that as such it may not be added to food products without specific approval from the FDA. Accordingly, allowing for the sale of existing stocks, any manufacturer or distributor of a food product in violation of this ruling thirty days after the date of this order will be assessed substantial fines for violating the Act.

Part C. At this point, your original clients (soft drink manufacturers and makers of caffeine additives) seek your advice on whether they now have grounds to bring suit against the FDA. They would like your advice on whether there are any procedural or substantive grounds for challenging the Commissioner's apparent order that they stop the use of caffeine in soft drinks and other food products and whether the Commissioner can be prevented from participating in further proceedings on the issue. Please write a memorandum concerning these issues.

SAMPLE ANSWER TO QUESTION 2

Part A. The first issue is whether there is a dispute that is ripe for review at this time. All the FDA has done is announce that it will take enforcement action in a category of cases in the future. It has not taken action against anyone yet. Assuming that judicial review is available for any enforcement order issued, there may not be any reason to allow judicial review at this time. Further, it is not clear what the FDA will actually do under the new statement, because the statement may be unfit for review. The FDA might be very strict and reject most applications, or it might be very liberal and grant most applications to use additives that occur naturally.

Assuming that review is available now, or perhaps later, there are several grounds for challenging the FDA's new policy. First, the manufacturers may argue that the policy statement is a legislative rule and should have been promulgated with a notice and comment process. This is not a very strong argument. The strongest argument for the challengers is that the FDA will act in the future as if it is bound to take action against caffeine and other similar additives. The new interpretation of the Act also adds to the law since the FDA claims the power to take enforcement action that it previously said it could not take. However, despite these arguments, when an agency announces its enforcement policy, it is considered a policy statement and does not have to use a notice and comment process. Further, this particular statement is arguably interpretative, since it construes the word "drug" and the terms of the agency's power to regulate food additives. A court on judicial review after an enforcement order might reject these interpretations, and the agency's statement is not a binding legal obligation until an enforcement order is actually issued and upheld on judicial review.

Another issue is whether the FDA's view that caffeine is a drug is consistent with the statute. Here, by not defining "drug," Congress probably left it to the FDA to fill in the gap. Under *Chevron,* Congress has not directly spoken to whether caffeine, or naturally occurring food ingredients generally, can be considered drugs. The question is whether the FDA's interpretation is permissible. Using a looser version of *Chevron* step one, if the legislative history of the statute reveals that Congress would not have wanted the FDA to regulate caffeine, then perhaps a court would overrule the agency. But it is likely that the FDA would be upheld, absent strong evidence of congressional intent to the contrary.

The next issue has to do with the extensive ex parte contacts that occurred prior to the issuance of the statement. Nothing in the APA prohibits these contacts. In fact, without any sort of notice and comment process, it is difficult to imagine any legal doctrine that would prevent the agency from having contacts with anyone it wants to. If there had been an actual rulemaking, then a court might have required the agency to place all the information it had on the record for comment. Insofar as the agency appears to be using the statements plus the threat of prosecution as a substitute for a rulemaking, some courts might be very suspicious of what the agency did. However, it is unclear whether anything could be done at this point. The whole process seems unfair, but there is no apparent remedy.

In sum, it is unlikely that a court would prevent the agency from conducting research and from issuing a policy statement that informs the public that it intends to prosecute certain cases in the future. Perhaps a rule on prosecutions would be unreviewable as committed to agency discretion by law. In any case, judicial review is not likely to be available until the agency brings an enforcement proceeding or promulgates a legislative rule.

Part B. These facts raise a claim of discriminatory enforcement. Jake Cola would argue that it is a patent abuse of discretion for the FDA to prosecute when Jake Cola has less caffeine than most other sodas and when its market share, even in its local area, is minuscule. The agency would have to articulate some reason for its choice. Courts are so deferential to agency enforcement priorities that the agency might be upheld if it says something as empty as "we chose this company as one of many that we ultimately intend to prosecute." Further, putting First Amendment concerns aside, the agency might rely upon a policy of prosecuting companies that mention caffeine, and could say "we are looking into whether we should bring an action against Jolt." However, if a court took the possibility of a discriminatory enforcement claim seriously, this should be a good case. There is no question that the other sodas have caffeine — unlike the *Universal-Rundle* case where the agency could say it was an open question whether the other companies were violating the law. However, on the other hand, it is not clear how badly Jake would be hurt if he cannot use caffeine. After all, he uses very little and there are colas without caffeine on the market.

It should be noted that the discriminatory-enforcement issue may not be ripe for review until the agency actually issues an order against Jake. There is no final order and no other obvious basis for immediate judicial review. There is neither fitness nor hardship. We don't really know what order, if any, will be issued; we also do not know what effect the order will have. The cost of defending is not sufficient hardship.

Part C. First, there is no problem with the agency reversing the ALJ since credibility is not an issue. The basis for the reversal is a matter of policy that the agency should be able to decide itself. The ALJ's discriminatory-enforcement decision is entitled to no deference from the agency. Although a court should take it into account on judicial review, it is purely an issue of policy, and the agency should be free to reverse it.

At this point, there is no ripeness problem since a final order has been issued. The discriminatory enforcement issue is ripe since a cease and desist order has been issued. The analysis in Part B should be applied to the claim.

There is also a question of standing. Do the other soft drink manufacturers or the caffeine producers have standing? It seems clear that the drink makers do have standing in that they are likely to be subjected to an order to change their product in the very near future. They are directly regulated, so the zone of interests is not an issue. The caffeine makers are injured directly by the agency action since the market for their product will shrink (and has already shrunk), but there is a zone of interests question since nothing in the FDA Act is concerned with the interests of ingredient makers. Further, they would be asserting the rights of third parties (the drink manufacturers) who are perfectly able to assert their own rights. Finally, their presence does not really add anything to the case. I would be inclined to allow them to have standing because it does not really hurt anything. They are clearly injured, but a strict court might deny them standing on the ground that they are asserting third party rights and are not within the zone of interests of the law in question.

The main question here is whether it is proper for the commissioner to include what looks like a rule about caffeine in his decision in the case about Jake. He says he will seek large fines in the future even though he has not fined Jake at all. Some members of the Court have thought this is fine since prospective rules are part of the judicial process. Others think it is fine because future subjects will be fined only after a hearing. The dissenters thought that if an agency wants to make a general rule, it should have to use the rulemaking procedure of the APA. In my view, the commissioner will be upheld. The rule announced here is about the particular additive caffeine. The FDA proceeds largely through enforcement actions. It seems appropriate, under *Bell Aerospace,* for it to decide case-by-case which additives will be treated as drugs. As long as future subjects are given hearings, I see nothing wrong with announcing a strong precedent in the course of an adjudication. Here, a retroactive rule would be worse than the prospective one, since the agency is at least warning people before it issues fines.

The question remains, however, whether the commissioner can announce this rule in an opinion and then rely on it in later prosecutions for levying fines. Here, if the commissioner does not explicitly state "I am assessing a large fine because the Jake Cola rule has been violated," there is not much of a problem. The commissioner should state that the fine is because of the violation found at the hearing. The commissioner will probably argue that he did not issue any rule in Jake Cola, he just stated what he intended to do in future cases. Those cases would still be decided on their own merits, and the violation would be for putting a drug in food, not for violating any aspect of the Jake Cola opinion.

The clients might argue that the Commissioner is biased or has prejudged the law in these cases and should not be allowed to sit on review of ALJ decisions. This argument sounds good, but it would basically destroy the system Congress has established for agency review of ALJ decisions. Agencies often announce rules and then sit as a reviewing tribunal. The agency is no more biased than a court that has announced a precedent and then has a later case on the same issue. Prejudgment raises the same issue. In order to win on this argument, there would have to be a showing that the commissioner is simply unwilling to even look at the evidence in the case. This looks more like the standard for prejudgment in a rulemaking. In effect, on policy decisions, the commissioner should be judged on the rulemaking standard to allow him to carry out the functions Congress has assigned. Just as some judges have clear views on issues, like the death penalty or separation of powers, the commissioner is free to express those views in cases as long as in subsequent cases the commissioner is willing to look at the evidence and weigh the arguments.

In sum, I do not see any basis for reversing the Commissioner or disqualifying him from hearing future cases.

QUESTION 3:   Since 1933 prices paid by handlers of milk to producers of milk have been set by the Secretary of Agriculture under what are denominated as Marketing Orders. Handlers, in turn, sell milk to food producers for use in prepared foods and to local dairies for public sale in retail stores. The Secretary's authority to establish Marketing Orders derives from the Agricultural Marketing Agreement Act. A section of this statute provides:

> The price of milk paid by milk handlers to milk producers shall be set by
> the Secretary, in his discretion, after hearing, to reflect the price of feeds, the
> available supplies of feeds, and other economic conditions which affect market
> supply and demand for milk or its products in the marketing area to which the

contemplated marketing agreement, order, or amendment relates. Whenever the Secretary in his discretion finds, upon the basis of the evidence adduced at the hearing required by this section that the price of milk is not reasonable in view of the price of feeds, the available supplies of feeds, and other economic conditions which affect market area supply and demand for milk in the marketing area, he shall fix such prices as he finds will reflect such factors, insure a sufficient quantity of pure and wholesome milk to meet current needs and further to assure a level of farm income adequate to maintain productive capacity sufficient to meet anticipated future needs, and be in the public interest. Thereafter, as the Secretary finds necessary on account of changed circumstances, he shall, after due notice and opportunity for hearing, make adjustments in such prices.

The reference to "marketing area" in this provision concerns the Secretary's statutory authority to divide the nation into regions and to issue different Marketing Orders for each. Under this authority the Secretary has delineated 40 marketing areas, and every time he has set a price that handlers must pay milk producers for milk to be sold in a marketing area east of the Rocky Mountains he has added a differential based on the distance of the center of the area from Eau Claire, Wisconsin, the hub of the nation's traditional milk-producing region. This differential was established after a notice and comment rulemaking in 1934. In this rulemaking the Secretary explained that he interpreted the phrase "other economic conditions" to include consideration of distance from the center of the nation's milk-producing region because places distant from this center were not receiving adequate supplies of milk. The Secretary stated that the distance-from-Eau Claire price differential would encourage the transportation of milk into all marketing areas. In 1935 a court of appeals held that the Secretary's rule was supported by substantial evidence and was not arbitrary and capricious.

Since the adoption of this pricing system, milk shortages have not occurred in any regions. During this period milk production also has become more dispersed in the Eastern United States, a dispersal that perhaps has been encouraged by the higher prices that milk handlers must pay for milk that is to be sold in regions more distant from Eau Claire. Nonetheless, the Secretary has not adjusted the pricing system, except periodically, through notice and comment rulemaking, to adjust for changes in the differential due to inflation in shipping costs.

Last year the Secretary issued a notice that he was considering a minor increase in milk prices to adjust for inflation. Consumer groups, milk handlers, dairy farmers in areas relatively close to Eau Claire, food producers in areas distant from Eau Claire, and retail grocery companies from around the country all commented that the entire system of setting milk prices is obsolete and that the reference to Eau Claire, Wisconsin, should be abandoned, because distance from this city has no relation to the actual cost of producing and supplying milk. Milk producers in areas distant from Eau Claire and others commented on other issues, but did not address the Eau Claire-based differential. Both camps of milk producers, however, heavily lobbied the Secretary and his assistants as well as members of Congress, expressing their contrasting views on the retention of the existing milk marketing order price structure.

The Secretary has now promulgated a regulation making the minor adjustments to milk prices he proposed last year. In an accompanying statement, the Secretary explained that the "existing pricing system is maintained with minor adjustments for inflation in shipping and other costs." The Secretary did not make findings on the specific economic factors listed in the statute and did not respond to the comments that argued that the traditional factors used in setting prices were obsolete.

Consumer groups, Wisconsin milk producers, and food producers in areas distant from Eau Claire would like to seek judicial review of the Secretary's failure to alter the system for setting milk prices. Analyze whether each of these groups has standing to seek such review. Then consider the merits of the arguments they might advance against the Secretary. Is the 1935 circuit court decision upholding the system relevant to any of these arguments? What other information would you like to have? (Ignore what you know about the actual regulation of milk pricing and the case on which this problem is based.)

SAMPLE ANSWER TO QUESTION 3

First, the standing of each group of potential plaintiffs should be addressed. The basic requirements for standing should be laid out, including injury traceable to the challenged conduct and redressability. Consumer groups have standing if members pay more for milk than under an alternative regulatory scheme they claim should replace the current scheme for milk pricing. Although many people share in the injury, because the price setting scheme probably increases the price of milk, consumer complaints should not fail based on the generalized grievance doctrine because the consumers of milk are suing over something that affects them directly based on particular market activity, not merely by virtue of being a member of society. There also should be a brief discussion of the requirements for associational standing. Wisconsin milk producers have standing because the system for setting milk prices affects them directly in that it prescribes the price they are paid for their product. Even if deregulation might ultimately hurt them if prices moved lower, they are now not able to compete for business based on price and that restriction is enough of an injury for standing. Food producers in areas distant from Eau Claire are injured because they pay more for milk than producers closer to Eau Claire which in turn hurts their ability to compete with food producers near Eau Claire. Thus, it appears that all the potential plaintiffs are injured sufficient for standing.

On the merits, this question raises a very interesting issue: If an agency takes an action, and that action has been upheld on judicial review, can changed circumstances render that action arbitrary and capricious or lacking in substantial evidence so that a challenge years after the action was upheld on judicial review could prevail? It appears that the substantial evidence test might apply here if the Secretary held a formal hearing. If not, review could still be had under the arbitrary and capricious test. Since it is not clear whether there really is a difference between the two tests when reviewing policy decisions of the sort at issue here, the specific test will be mentioned only when it might make a difference.

One issue might be reviewability, since the statute says that the Secretary shall make changes "as the Secretary finds necessary." This looks like a deeming clause in that it appears to vest substantial discretion in the Secretary. However, this type of phrasing is not sufficient to overcome the presumption in favor of judicial review. From what the facts indicate, action under this program has been subjected to judicial review since at least 1935. The same phrase also says that under certain circumstances the Secretary "shall" make adjustments to milk prices, indicating a legally enforceable obligation to do so. Further, there is no basis for holding this as unreviewable prosecutorial discretion since the statute states pretty clearly when the Secretary is required to act.

Turning to the merits, the challenge is really not to the failure to act for 60 years, but the latest action which the Secretary took, i.e., making minor adjustments to milk prices when the comments urged the Secretary to make substantial changes based on changed circumstances, which is exactly what the statute appears to tell the Secretary to do. Here, the question is whether, based on everything in the record, a reasonable person could have reached this conclusion (substantial evidence) or whether the Secretary considered the relevant factors, applied the correct legal standard, and made a clear error in judgment (arbitrary and capricious). It would be useful to have more information about what information exactly the record contains. Further, there may be a procedural problem since the Secretary did not address the major issue of the obsolescence of the pricing system in the concise general statement and did not make findings on the issues specified in the statute. While formal findings are not required, courts can insist on a reasoned explanation of major statutory and policy issues in the concise general statement without violating *Vermont Yankee*'s prohibition on additional procedural requirements.

The fact that a court, in 1935, upheld this pricing system does not answer whether it is error for the Secretary to issue an order maintaining the 1935 system in light of today's circumstances. While a court might be reluctant to hold that an agency must revise regulations periodically to adjust for changing conditions, here the statute itself, and thus Congress, requires revision, so the 1935 decision should not really matter.

The final issue is ex parte contacts. Although the facts are not very specific, it appears that there was a great deal of lobbying going on from both sides. Some courts have held that ex parte contacts should not occur. If this was a formal adjudicatory hearing or a formal rulemaking, the ex parte contacts would present a reason under the APA to send the matter back to the agency for a new decision. Ex parte contacts are forbidden in such proceedings. If this was informal rulemaking, nothing in the APA prohibits ex parte contacts. Some courts have prohibited them, especially when the rulemaking resolves a competing claim to a valuable privilege, but this may violate *Vermont Yankee* by imposing a procedural requirement not contained in the APA. The court could say that it is merely enforcing §553 by giving everyone an equal, adequate opportunity to participate in the rulemaking, but it is unclear whether the Supreme Court would accept this. More in keeping with *Vermont Yankee,* agencies in informal rulemaking can probably receive ex parte contacts but should place any important information on the record. As long as there is no suggestion that ex parte contacts involved irrelevant factors such as funding of other agency projects, etc., a system that allows ex parte contacts in rulemaking is probably better than one that attempts to prohibit them.

As a last comment, it should be noted that the agency might have run into trouble had it decided in this proceeding to radically alter the milk pricing system. It is not altogether clear that the interests in favor of preserving the system were aware that this was a possibility raised by some of the comments. Perhaps they were since they did support their interests in ex parte contacts. But the notice did not raise the possibility, and if an agency wants to make a substantial change to longstanding practice, it should probably provide better notice than it did in this case, so that any change will not materially alter the proposal, or not be a logical outgrowth of the proposal. Otherwise, interested parties might not realize that they should comment to protect their interests.

QUESTION 4:   [This question is fictional, and no environmental statutes not referred to in the question should be consulted.]

The Environmental Protection Agency (EPA) is concerned about air pollution resulting from the evaporation of gasoline fumes at gas stations. Under its statutory power to "issue such rules and regulations it finds to be reasonably necessary to protect the human environment," it has issued a notice of proposed rulemaking which states:

> EPA is seeking to reduce or eliminate the evaporation of fumes at gasoline stations. Many options are being considered, including, but not limited to, a recovery device on automobiles and/or a recovery device on gasoline pumps.

In response to this notice, EPA received hundreds of comments. Many comments stated that recovery devices on automobiles would be unsafe and expensive and that recovery devices on pumps would be ineffective and expensive. Several comments, from environmental groups, advocated a reformulation of gasoline that would significantly lower the rate of evaporation and thus would accomplish EPA's goal without any device at all. These comments also argued that gasoline reformulation was the cheapest method of reducing fumes.

After reviewing the comments, EPA issued a regulation requiring, within six months, that all gasoline sold in the United States conform to the reformulation as proposed in the comments.

The Oil Companies were not pleased with this action. They claim they did not have adequate notice or opportunity to comment on this regulation. They have filed petitions for judicial review of the regulation in the appropriate federal court. They also have lobbied Congress for statutory relief and they have lobbied the President to overturn the regulation.

The efforts in Congress failed, but just before the regulation was to go into effect, the President issued an Executive Order suspending the effect of the regulation "until such time as the EPA conducts a thorough reassessment of the regulation in light of the costs the regulation would impose on the oil industry." Environmental groups and automobile manufacturers have sued the EPA seeking an order that the regulation be enforced as written. They argue that the suspension of the regulation is illegal presidential interference with the EPA's rulemaking authority.

You are a law clerk to the judge before whom both cases have been consolidated. Please write a memorandum with your opinion on the cases. He is most interested in whether the APA has been violated and whether the President's action raises constitutional or statutory issues. Do not worry about whether the Oil Company challenge is moot — another clerk is working on that issue.

SAMPLE ANSWER TO QUESTION 4

The two biggest issues in this problem are notice and presidential power to order an agency to suspend a regulation and do cost-benefit analysis.

The main notice problem is that the notice of proposed rulemaking did not mention the possibility that the agency would require reformulated gasoline. The only possibilities actually mentioned were vapor recovery devices on gasoline pumps or in cars. The oil companies will argue they did not have sufficient notice. They will stress the purposes of the notice requirement (giving parties a meaningful opportunity to comment and ensuring the agency receives useful information) and argue that neither of these purposes were served since the oil companies had no idea that reformulation of gasoline was being considered.

In my view, these notice arguments should fail for several reasons. First, the agency was careful to say that it was considering many options, not limited to the ones mentioned. The oil companies should have realized their product might be affected since it was their product that was causing the environmental problem. Second, the agency complied with the terms of the APA, §553. Section 553 requires notice of the terms of the proposed rule *or* the subjects or issues involved. The notice definitely included the subjects or issues involved in the rulemaking. After *Vermont Yankee,* courts should not add to APA procedural requirements, and since the agency complied with §553, there should be no notice issue. Third, basing the argument on the "opportunity to comment" should not help turn a bad notice argument into one based more firmly on the terms of §553. All notice problems affect the opportunity to comment, and as long as the notice meets the notice requirements of §553, a court should not use a different provision to void the rulemaking.

The EPA may argue that based on the language of the statute, the decision of how much to regulate is committed to agency discretion by law. The statute looks like a "deeming clause" in that it says that the EPA should issue regulations that "it *finds* to be reasonably necessary." While in some contexts this might indicate intent to vest the agency with unreviewable discretion, this kind of language is used all the time and is not sufficient to overcome the presumption in favor of judicial review. The statute is a typical regulatory statute and gives plenty of guidance to facilitate judicial review.

There also is a ripeness issue here because the companies want to challenge a rule before it has been enforced against them. They need to meet the fitness and hardship test to get judicial review before agency enforcement. Here, there probably is hardship. Whatever it costs to reformulate, including potential costs to modify refineries and do all the research and testing to make the new gasoline work properly, cause plenty of hardship. The issue also may be fit for judicial review because there are really no individualized issues, just the question whether the agency had a sufficient basis to require the reformulation based on the facts in the record and also whether the agency observed all required procedures. It is not a purely legal issue like *Abbott Laboratories* but the decision does not vary from company to company based on the situation, so the rule is fit for review at this time.

The second set of issues concerns the President's order suspending the regulation and requiring EPA to reconsider in light of the costs of the regulation. I want to clear away one issue I think is a red herring first, that of ex parte contacts. It could be argued that the oil companies did something wrong by approaching the President outside the notice and comment process. I think any suggestion that this was improper should be rejected. In a democracy, contact with elected officials is to be expected and in fact valued. Nothing in the APA limits this type of contact, and it might even be unconstitutional to attempt to prevent the President from having contact with members of the public who are interested in a matter before an agency.

The President's order raises a whole set of interesting questions. First, there is the question of the President's inherent power to supervise the executive branch. EPA is an executive agency. The President has the power to fire the administrator of the EPA, and presumably if the President cannot convince an EPA administrator to delay the effective date of a regulation, the President could fire the person and appoint someone more responsive. If you believe the unitary executive theory, the fact that Congress delegated the authority directly to the EPA should not matter, because any effort to prevent presidential influence is unconstitutional. If you take a more moderate view, and hold that the President's power is merely to execute the laws as written by Congress, then you would be more troubled by presidential intervention into the EPA's work. Sure the President could fire the administrator, but he may not want to do so for a variety of reasons, and he should not be able to meddle in authority delegated to the administrator. If Congress has not specifically denied the President the power to suspend regulations, and also has not granted the power, the question falls into Justice Jackson's middle category and raises a difficult, uncertain question. This separation of powers issue is not governed directly by caselaw, so I am not able here to resolve it authoritatively, and leave open the question whether the President has this power.

Coming at the issue from another angle, the question may be whether it violates separation of powers for Congress to delegate power directly to the EPA and not allow the President to directly supervise the EPA's decisions. Unless you believe in the unitary executive theory, this question should be answered under general separation of powers standards which would ask whether the President's ability to carry out his constitutional role or function as an independent branch of government is threatened. Again, unless you believe in the unitary executive, insulation from direct presidential supervision should be upheld. The President has no interest in enforcing the law except as written by Congress, and this law grants the discretion to the EPA.

There is another serious problem with the President's order. The President ordered EPA to reassess its decision in light of the costs to the oil industry. The question is whether cost to the oil industry is a relevant factor that the agency should consider. (I am putting to one side the very uncertain issue of whether the President can order the agency to consider a factor that it would prefer not to consider but which may be within a permissible construction of the statute. That issue is subsumed in the discussion above.) The statute says "reasonably necessary to protect the human environment." The use of the words "reasonably necessary" has been held, in the OSH Act, not to require cost-benefit analysis, and the EPA may interpret this to consider environmental protection only, and not costs. If Congress did not intend for the agency to consider costs, then any rule considering them would be arbitrary and capricious for considering an irrelevant factor. The President does not have the power to amend a statute. If a court finds that Congress did not intend for costs to be considered, then the President would not have the power to order the agency to consider them.

There is an argument that the President should have the rather moderate power to order an agency to rethink a regulation in light of issues that the President finds important. Further, it can be argued that since the regulation had not yet gone into effect, it is not a big step for the President to ask for a delay. However, this ignores the fact that the agency had promulgated the requirement as a final rule. In the *Airbags* case, the Court held that an agency could not just throw out a final rule without good reason, and in that case the rule had not yet gone into effect. By analogy, this rule is entitled to all the respect afforded a rule that has actually gone into effect. The President cannot by fiat suspend the operation of a validly promulgated rule.

Finally, standing should be mentioned. The environmental groups would have to establish injury. They can probably do that just by alleging that some of their members breathe the air that is affected by gasoline vapors. The groups would have to meet the requirements for associational standing: Members must be injured, the claim must be related to the association's purpose, and participation of individuals must be unnecessary to resolution of the case. These factors are likely to be present here.

In sum, the EPA probably gave sufficient notice, and the President's order raises serious questions regarding presidential power to supervise agencies.

Table of Cases

This table includes references to cases cited everywhere in this book, including
the various Exam Q&A sections.

149

Index

This index includes references to the Capsule Summary and to the
Exam Tips, but not to Q&A or Flow Charts